新东方
NEW ORIENTAL

CW01669194

Master IELTS

IELTS WRITE RIGHT

IELTS 9分写作

编著／Julian Charles

西安交通大学出版社
XI'AN JIAOTONG UNIVERSITY PRESS

图书在版编目(CIP)数据

IELTS 9 分写作 / (澳)查尔斯(Charles, J.)编著.
西安：西安交通大学出版社，2008.8
ISBN 978-7-5605-2914-1

Ⅰ. I… Ⅱ. 查… Ⅲ. 英语—写作—高等教育—自学参考资料 Ⅳ. H315

中国版本图书馆 CIP 数据核字（2008）第 119743 号

版权登记：陕版出图字 25 - 2008 - 038

书　　名	IELTS 9 分写作
编 著 者	(澳)Julian Charles
责任编辑	谭小艺　李小艾
封面设计	大愚设计
出版发行	西安交通大学出版社
地　　址	西安市兴庆南路 10 号(邮编:710049)
电　　话	(029)82668357　82667874(发行部)
	(029)82668315　82669096(总编办)
印　　刷	北京鑫丰华彩印有限公司
字　　数	283 千
开　　本	787×1092　1/16
印　　张	20.25
版　　次	2008 年 9 月第 1 版　2008 年 9 月第 1 次印刷
书　　号	ISBN 978-7-5605-2914-1/H・816
定　　价	40.00 元

How to use this book

Introduction 本书简介

IELTS Write Right is intended to assist you, the IELTS candidate, in expanding your repertoire of sentence structures, improving your coherence and cohesion and extending your range of vocabulary with a view to achieving better results in the IELTS writing section. By providing alternate model answers to IELTS writing tasks, it provides a framework within which you can discover for yourself many of the important stylistic differences between everyday English and English as it is used in academic writing.

《IELTS 9 分写作》可帮助考生全面提升 IELTS 写作能力，包括增加词汇使用的广度，加强句子的连贯性和文章的流畅度。而本书提供的写作范文，更可帮助读者分辨日常生活用语与学术写作英文的差异，轻松取得 IELTS 高分。

IELTS Band Scores 参考分数

IELTS is designed to test the English ability of non-native speakers. However, the model answers in this book are written by a native speaker, with none of the mistakes that an IELTS candidate might make. Therefore, it is very difficult to evaluate the quality of the model answers in this book using IELTS band scores. It is important that you remember the IELTS band scores in this text are included as a general guide only and are simply intended to help you to identify better ways of writing.

本书所提供的写作范文，皆由母语为英文的外国人士所撰写，旨在为读者提供写作学习的范本，范文的分数仅供参考。

Model Answers 写作范文

Two model answers are provided for every question in this book. Compare them and try to find different (and more stylistically complex) ways to write. Remember that easy is not always best. In each case Model Answer A is easier to understand and will show you how to organise your essay; however, Model Answer B is an example of better writing. Therefore, you should try to base your own writing on Model Answer B (Note: Questions 28, 29 and 30 are exceptions to this rule as they are examples of informal letter writing).

本书的每个问题皆提供两篇写作范文，考生可比较两篇文章的差异，并试着自己练习写作。其中 Model A 比较简单，考生可以参考其组织架构；而 Model B 是高分范文，考生可学习其句型和用词。

Model Sentence Structures 句型示范

To succeed in IELTS writing you must learn to write complex and varied sentence structures. The "***Model Sentence Structures***" sections included after each pair of model answers will help you to do this. These sections demonstrate how to convert a simple sentence into academic English. For example:

Basic sentence

Sentence 1	**IELTS 5**	The graph shows some similarities between the birth rates of China and the USA from 1920 to 2000.
	IELTS 6	The graph provided reveals some surprising similarities between the Chinese and US birth rates during the period from 1920 to 2000.
	IELTS 7⁺	A glance at the graph provided reveals some striking similarities between the Chinese and US birth rates during the period from 1920 to 2000.

Intermediate sentence

Advanced sentence

"***Show***" and "***reveal***" mean the same thing, but "***reveal***" is a better word to use. Similarly, "***the graph shows***" is not bad, but "***a glance at the graph provided reveals***" is much better. Aim for the target.

写作要拿到高分，一定要会使用一些较复杂的句子。本书的"句型示范"提供5分、6分和7分以上三个层次的句子，指导考生如何写出可拿高分的句子。

Academic Vocabulary 高分词汇

Synonyms, like "***get***" and "***receive***", are words that mean the same thing. Learning synonyms improves your writing. You probably already know a lot of vocabulary to use when speaking; however, to achieve a higher band score in IELTS writing you should try to learn more formal, academic vocabulary. Tables of synonyms are provided after each pair of model answers to assist you in identifying these.

Also, you should not use a word just because it is easy to remember or because you already know it. Extend your repertoire! For example, "***sharp***" is a very basic word and one that many IELTS candidates use, while "***exponential***" sounds much more formal and is used by fewer candidates. In many cases, you will need to use basic vocabulary; however, you should use intermediate or advanced vocabulary wherever possible.

要多学一些同义词。一些在口语中经常使用的词汇，如果用在 IELTS 写作中，并不容易拿高分。在 IELTS 写作测试中应该多使用较正式的、学术性的词汇。本书的"高分词汇"收集了基础、中级和高级词汇，帮助考生学习同义词的表达，运用高级词汇，迈向写作高分。

Basic 基础 5+分	**Intermediate 中级** 6+分	**Advanced 高级** 7+分
increase (v.)	rise (v.) climb (v.)	
sharp (adj.)	dramatic (adj.)	exponential (adj.)

Test Your Comprehension 综合练习

The comprehension questions included are designed to draw your attention to various important features of the model answers and to extend your understanding of them. Among other things, they will test your comprehension of factual information, your ability to arrange ideas in a logical sequence, your grasp of English grammar and your ability to distinguish between spoken and written English vocabulary. Be sure to complete these questions after reading the model answers, model sentence structures and academic vocabulary sections. They will help you to judge whether or not you have gained the maximum benefit possible from the model answers.

"综合练习"除了可帮助读者充分掌握写作范文的重点外，还可帮助读者学习如何组织文章架构，练习语法以及学习写作词汇。

About IELTS

IELTS(International English Language Testing System)“国际英语语言测试系统”是全球认可的英语语言能力评估系统，也是进入大多数英语系国家高等学府就读必备的英语能力证明，特别受到英国、澳大利亚、新西兰、加拿大等国认可，而目前美国大多数大学也承认 IELTS 成绩。IELTS 测试由英国文化协会(The British Council)、剑桥大学考试委员会(Cambridge ESOL)及澳大利亚教育国际开发署(IDP Education Australia)共同举办，由剑桥大学考试委员会统筹管理。除了计划前往英语系国家就读大学、研究生院、专科技术学院、预科课程者适合参加 IELTS 测试外，凡申请澳大利亚、新西兰、加拿大、美国移民者，或是担任英国及澳洲各政府部门实习生、参加国防部及公共医疗会议等专业人士，均可参加 IELTS 测试。

IELTS 测试方式

IELTS 测试分为学术类（Academic）和培训类（General Training），测试内容分为听、读、说、写四部分，其中 Listening 和 Speaking 部分不分类，Reading 和 Writing 两项则分类。

■ 学术类(Academic)

适用于申请正规课程者，例如研究生院、大学、专科学校或要求此类者。

■ 培训类(General Training)

适用于申请移民者及欲申请学校要求此类者。

IELTS 测试流程图

IELTS测试分为听力、阅读、写作、口语四部分，测试时间为2小时55分钟。

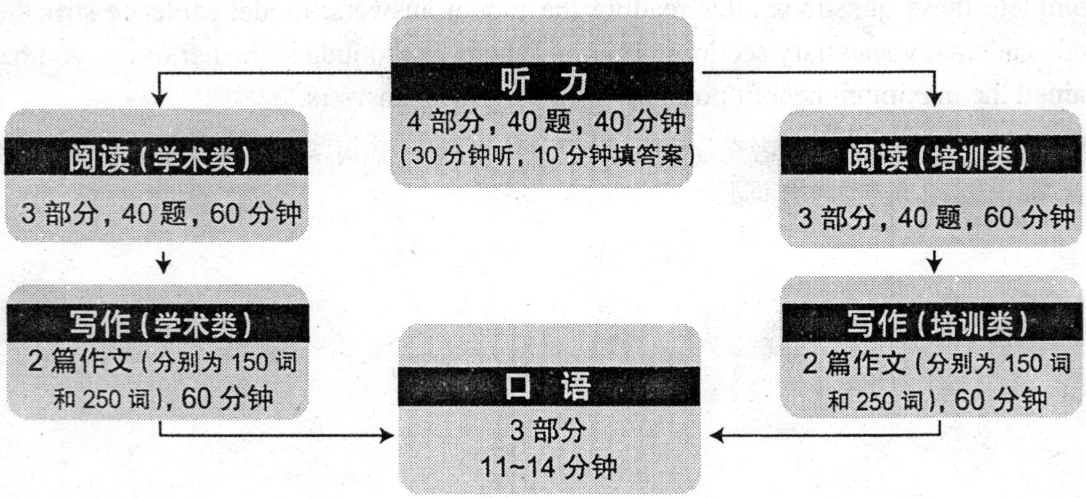

IELTS 测试内容

■ IELTS Listening Module·听力

内容	·测试时间 40 分钟，其中 10 分钟填答案 ·分为 4 部分，共有 40 题 ·听力只放一遍，不会重复
题型结构	·第一、二段：以一般生活及社会状态为主 ·第三、四段：涵盖教育、学术、世界性的主题 ·题型：选择题、填空题、简答题、图表题
作答重点	·要边听边作答 ·需了解独白或对话的主题 ·注意数字、时间、日期等较明显的字眼 ·听出重要的词句，记下与主题相关或有因果关系的信息

■ IELTS Reading Module·阅读

内容	·测试时间 1 小时，含填写答案时间 ·包含 3 篇文章，每篇约有 800～900 词 ·测试题目共 40 题
题型结构	·主题多样化，除了日常生活，还包括学术上的探讨与了解 ·题型：简答题、选择题、匹配题、填空题、图表题、表格题、段落大意题、摘要题、是 / 非 / 未提及题（True/False/Not Given）
作答重点	·了解各段落主题与大意 ·圈出重要信息 ·圈出数字、日期、时间、项目等较明显的词句 ·不需要了解每一个单词的意思，不要浪费时间推敲不明白的地方

■ IELTS Writing Module · 写作

内容	· 测试时间 1 小时，需写 2 篇作文 · Task 1：最少 150 词，建议花 20 分钟 · Task 2：最少 250 词，建议花 40 分钟
题型结构	· Task 1：考题基本形式为图片、表格、曲线、饼状图等，考生依照所给的信息，分析、组织并讨论主题 · Task 2：依照所给的主题，表达自己的意见、支持或反驳、解决问题及讨论问题
作答重点	Task 1： · 避免使用自己没把握的单词和语法结构 · 从题目要求中，清楚分析题目，圈出重要的词或短语 Task 2： · 仔细阅读题目，避免文不对题 · 强调自己的想法和意见 · 支持或反对考题的论点，只能二选一，定位要清楚

■ IELTS Speaking Module · 口试

内容	· 测试时间约11～14分钟，分成3个部分 Part 1：4～5分钟，自我介绍及面谈 Part 2：3～4分钟，1分钟准备，对特定话题发表看法 Part 3：4～5分钟，第二部分的延伸讨论，题目较第二部分抽象
题型结构	· Part 1：口试官介绍自己并确认考生身份，询问考生与个人有关的事物、家人、兴趣、工作背景等 · Part 2：口试官出示话题卡，考生依据话题卡可有1分钟的准备时间，考场备有纸笔供考生使用 · Part 3：连结第二部分的延伸讨论，或更深更广的互动讨论
作答重点	· 有效表达意见，与口试官沟通 · 正确使用词汇和语法 · 能够参与一般对话或勇于发问、发言 · 轻松应对，表达流畅，答为所问

IELTS 测试的一天

■ 笔试部分

时　间	考场建议
在早上8:00前 到达考场	· 请在考试当天上午8:00前到达考试中心。8:30以后停止进场。8:30以后到达考场的考生将被取消参加笔试的资格，并不得转考、退考或退费。笔试迟到的考生有权利选择参加口语考试。 · 在考场张贴的名单上找到自己的名字，记住自己的考场。 · 听从考试中心工作人员的指挥到候考室候考。 · 仔细听考试中心的工作人员介绍考前的注意事项。
入场 上午8:00 到 8:30	· 遵照考试中心工作人员的安排在教室外按照考号顺序排队等候。请在排队前先上洗手间。 · 在进入教室前准备好您的身份证和一张护照尺寸的彩照待检。彩照必须是六个月内的近照，且背面要写上您的名字。请将您的私人物品存放在指定的区域。 · 根据桌上的标签找到您的位置。 · 请就座。您可以利用这段时间测试一下您的耳机。
准备考试 上午8:30 到 9:00	· 在所有考生就坐后，监考人员会开始宣读考试事项。 · 您的身份证会被暂时集中收起，并在笔试结束前发还给您。 · 监考人员会给您分发听力/阅读答题纸。请根据指示填好答题纸(听力部分和阅读部分的答题区分别在答题纸的正反两面)。 · 根据指示测试您的耳机。 · 监考人员将分发听力试卷并要求您在封面填写姓名和考号。 · 听力考试录音带中会提示您何时打开试卷。在此之前，您不可以打开试卷。 · 在考试正式开始以前，监考人员还会要求您再次检查耳机。
考试进行中 上午9:00到12:00	· 考试于早上9:00正式开始。 · 请注意听从监考人员的指示。 · 如果您有疑问，请举手向监考人员示意寻求帮助。 · 如果您认为您得到的试卷有误，或是试卷缺页、模糊，请马上告诉监考人员。 · 在考试进行期间，您不能和其他考生互借文具。 · 当您听到停止作答的指示时，请马上停止答卷，并放下铅笔。否则您将被视为违反考试规则，可能被取消考试成绩。

■ 口试部分

- 请在您预定的口试时间前 30 分钟到达考试中心并签到。未能在考试前 15 分钟到达并签到的考生，将有可能被取消参加口试的资格，并不得转考、退考或退费。
- 请带上您的身份证参加口试。
- 听从工作人员的指挥，在候考室待考。工作人员会带领您到口试考场。请在口试考场外等候考官请您进入。
- 口试考试时间为 11 到 14 分钟。
- 在完成口试后，请立即离开考场。不要与任何人谈及您的考试情况，否则可能会被视作违反考场纪律。

■ 考试建议

- 您可以在考试日前2个工作日从NEEA IELTS 报名网站(http://ielts.etest.net.cn)上查看您的考号和口试时间。
- 请您在参加考试前仔细阅读中国地区IELTS考生须知。
- 请您带上身份证明，一张护照尺寸的六个月内的彩照（照片后面附上您的签名)，以及您的准考证到考场。
- 您在笔试和口试入场前均须出示与报名时一致的有效身份证件，出示与报名信息不符证件的考生将有可能不能参加考试，并不得转考、退考或退费。
- 强烈建议您不要携带手机或其他电子通讯类产品进入考场。所有电子、通讯设备禁止带入考场，即使已呈关闭状态。这一规定同时适用于笔试和口试。任何携带电子、通讯设备进入考场的考生，一律取消考试资格。
- 除了需要检验身份证和照片之外，考生禁止携带任何私人物品进入考场。此规定同时适用于笔试和口试。请不要携带任何贵重物品到考场，考生的个人物品将被存放在考场以外的指定地点。英国文化协会(在中国作为英国使/领馆文化教育处开展工作)和考试中心恕不对考生个人物品的损失或遗失负责。

IELTS 测试成绩计算方式

IELTS 测试分为 Listening、Reading、Writing 和 Speaking 四项，此四项皆独立计分，最后再以四个分数合计，除以四而得一平均分数，所以在成绩单上会列出每项的分数和平均分数。IELTS 的满分为 9 分，若成绩达 Band 9，表示该考生能自如地运用英语，具备在英语语言国家学习的能力。反之，若成绩是 Band 1，则表示该考生不具有在英语语言国家学习的英语能力。每所学术机构要求的最低入学成绩不尽相同，一般来说，大部分学校会要求学生至少具备 IELTS 6.0~6.5 或同等程度的入学标准。

■ 计算方式

四大项都有 0.5 分(如 5.5,6.5)。

总分：将四项得分平均后，除 0.5 分外，每 0.25 进一个单位(0.5)

	例一	例二	例三
听力 Listening Band	7.5	6.0	6.0
阅读 Reading Band	6.5	6.0	5.5
写作 Writing Band	6.0	7.0	6.0
口试 Speaking Band	7.0	7.0	5.0
平均	(7.5+6.5+6.0+7.0)/4 =6.75(可进位)	(6.0+6.0+7.0+7.0)/4 =6.5	(6.0+5.5+6.0+5.0)/4 =5.625(不可进位)
总分	7	6.5	5.5

■ 寄送成绩

测试成绩将于考试后10个工作日寄送给考生。如成绩不理想，可随时再次报考。此规定适用于全球考试中心。

■ 成绩复议

若欲复议成绩，需在考后收到成绩单一个月内，由本人携带成绩单原件至原考试中心填写“成绩复议申请表”，缴复议费用900元，申请机构收到申请表后，在8周内通知复议结果，超过一个月才申请复议将不予受理。

若复议结果高于原成绩，则复议费用全数退还；若成绩相同或低于原分数，则复议费用不予退还。

■ IELTS测试成绩单申请办法

考生只能保留一份原始成绩单，成绩单由英国文化协会中国办公室（英国驻华使/领馆文化教育处）考试部在考试后的10个工作日内寄出。同时，该考试部将在考生考试日期之后一个月内为考生免费寄送 5 份额外的雅思考试成绩单。考生可以在报名考试时在教育部考试中心雅思报名网站 http://ielts.etest.net.cn 填写报名表时直接申请寄送，也可以在考试之后提交书面寄送申请。寄送申请必须在免费寄送期限内抵达相应的英国文化协会中国办公室考试部，如果考生在免费寄送期限之后提出寄送申请，每份成绩单需交纳手续费 60 元。如果考生需邮寄多于 5份的成绩单，超过的成绩单也需收取手续费 60 元。

CONTENTS

Master IELTS 5
IELTS WRITE RIGHT 9分写作

CONTENTS

IELTS

WRITE RIGHT

IELTS 写作常见问题和评分标准

IELTS FAQs & Writing Band Descriptors

Frequently Asked Questions

IELTS 写作常见问题

1. What do I have to write about in the IELTS writing section?

IELTS 写作测试的内容是什么?

All IELTS candidates must write two short essays: Writing Task 1 and Writing Task 2. If you wish to study abroad you must complete the IELTS Academic Module, in which you will be required to write a 150-word essay describing a graph, table or diagram (Task 1) together with a 250-word essay expressing your opinion on a set topic (Task 2). If, on the other hand, you wish to migrate to an English-speaking country, you must complete the General Training Module. This involves writing a 150-word letter (Task 1) along with a 250-word essay similar to that completed by Academic Module candidates (Task 2). A total of one hour is allowed for the completion of both writing tasks. Candidates are encouraged to spend about 20 minutes on Task 1 and 40 minutes on Task 2. In order to achieve a high score, it is important that both tasks be answered well.

IELTS 写作测试可以分为学术类和培训类，都包括TASK 1和TASK 2两部分(分别需要写150词和250词)。欲前往国外留学者须报考学术类，测试题型包括图表题及长篇写作题；而欲移民者须报考培训类，测试题型包括写一封信及一篇长篇文章。写作时间为1小时，建议TASK 1和TASK 2写作的分配时间分别为20分钟和40分钟。

2. How does the examiner decide what band score to give me?

阅卷者如何评分?

In IELTS writing the lowest band score is 1 and the highest band score is 9. Most candidates can expect to get a score of between 4 and 7. In marking your writing, the examiner will firstly check to see whether or not you have answered the question—if you are asked to write 250 words about air pollution in cities, you should not write 150 words about side issues such as traffic problems. The examiner will then check whether or not your essay is cohesive and coherent—your ideas, sentences and paragraphs must be logically organised and linked. He/she will also assess your grammar—you must use a variety of different grammatical forms and use them accurately. Finally, the examiner will assess your vocabulary—you must use a wide range of vocabulary and ensure that it is appropriate to the task set. In most cases, you will be expected to use formal, academic English.

写作测试的得分最低为1分，最高为9分。大部分考生的成绩介于4分到7分之间。回答是否切题为阅卷者首先关注的重点，接着阅卷者会审视考生的观点是否合乎逻辑，句子及段间的连接是否流畅，最后会检查考生是否运用了各种不同的语法结构并使用广泛的词汇。另外，应该尽量使用较正式、学术性的英文。

3. What happens if my essay isn't long enough?

如果写得太少会怎么样？

Length is certainly important; you should aim for 150 words in Task 1 and 250 words in Task 2. However, this should not be your main focus. It is still possible to attain a high score if you write a little less than this. Your grammar, vocabulary and spelling, as well as the way you organise your ideas, are more important. 230 well-written and logically organised words will get a better score than 330 poorly written words.

考生要尽量在TASK 1写到150词，在TASK 2写到250词；然而字数的多寡并非评分的主要重点，稍微少于题目要求的字数还是有可能拿到高分的。语法的运用、词汇的选择以及观点的组织才是得分的关键。

4. What should I do if I don't have any ideas about the topic?

若我对题目没有想法怎么办？

One problem faced by many candidates is lack of ideas, especially in Writing Task 2. It is very difficult indeed to write an essay about a topic you have never considered before. While most IELTS text books will tell you that no specialised knowledge is required to complete the IELTS writing section, many Writing Task 2 questions are underpinned by peculiarly western cultural concepts. It is, therefore, beneficial for candidates from Asian countries to have a broad knowledge of western social issues before taking IELTS. One thing that can help you to gain a deeper understanding of relevant issues is to research information related to known IELTS writing topics online. You might also try reading feature articles, editorials or letters to the editor in western newspapers and magazines.

IELTS 写作测试的TASK 2常出现以西方文化为观点的题目，所以越熟悉西方社会的议题对考生就越有帮助。其中一个办法是上网找一些与IELTS写作主题相关的资料，或者多阅读外国报纸或杂志上的文章或评论，以增进自己理解题目及组织观点的能力。

5. What happens if the examiner doesn't agree with me?

若阅卷者不同意我的观点怎么办?

You will not get a lower score if the examiner disagrees with you. IELTS is a test of your English not your opinion, so do not be scared to say what you think. Make sure you give reasons for your opinion, though. For example, you might write, "***I think we should discourage people from driving cars because cars cause pollution***". Also, make sure your reasons are logical. Many candidates write meaningless statements like, "***I think we should discourage people from driving cars because too many people drive cars***". Finally, remember that in western countries, disagreeing with people is acceptable and, in fact, often expected.

考生并不会因观点与阅卷者不一致得到较低的分数，因为IELTS是测试考生的英文水平而非考生的意见。在说英语的国家，反驳对方的意见通常是可被接受甚至是理所当然的，所以考生应勇于表达自己的观点，但记得要提供充分的理由支持你的观点。

6. Should I try to memorise lots of model answers?

我应该背诵写作范文吗?

No! Memorising vocabulary and sentence structures is certainly important. However, you should not try to memorise whole model answers and hope to be given a familiar topic when you take the test. Memorised answers are obvious to the examiner and usually receive a bad score. It is better to familiarise yourself with the sentence structures and patterns used in several different model answers and then combine them in your own way so that your writing is both natural and different from the writing of other candidates.

不要! 背单词和句型很重要，但不要背诵整篇范文，那样通常会拿到很低的分数。较好的方式为整合各种范例句型，尝试用自己的方式表达，与众不同的表达方式才是得高分的关键。

7. How can I get a higher score in IELTS writing?

要如何拿到高分？

Read read read read! You should read as many different model answers as you can, borrow sentence structures from each and then combine them in your own way. Rather than learning individual, isolated items of vocabulary you should try to learn them in the context of whole sentences. If you learn what a word means but do not know how to use it correctly in a sentence it is useless to you. Likewise, if you learn a sentence structure but omit a preposition or use the wrong verb tense, it will not improve your score. Your writing must be accurate.

多阅读。多阅读各种范文，然后整合其中的句型。不要单独背单词，试着从句子中学习词汇，这样你才会知道如何将其正确地运用在写作中。而套用句型时，同时要注意是否使用了正确的介词或动词时态。唯有精准的写作，才能得到高分。

8. Can I ask to have my writing marked again if I don't get the score I need?

如果得分不如预期的，可以复查吗？

You can ask to have your writing rechecked, but you have to pay an extra fee for this. Rechecking is only worthwhile if your overall band score is just a little lower than the band score that you need.

可以。但需要支付额外的复查费用。

IELTS Writing Task 1 Band Descriptors

IELTS 写作TASK 1 评分标准

You might be a little confused about what the IELTS writing band scores actually mean. What does it mean to get 6 in writing? How do examiners decide what score to give you? If your grammar is good, but your spelling is bad, what score will you get? There is no easy answer to any of these questions. However, to help you understand a little more about the IELTS marking system, the following have been included. They are the public versions of the *British Council / IDP Australia / University of Cambridge* Writing Task 1 and 2 band descriptors.

The language in the descriptors is hard to understand, and the difference between different band scores is not always clear (even to native English speakers). However the important thing to remember is that the IELTS examiners will check the following four aspects of your writing:

1. ***Task achievement:*** Did you answer the question that they asked you or did you talk about something else?

2. ***Coherence and cohesion:*** Does your writing make sense? Is your essay logically organised at the sentence, paragraph and whole text level?

3. ***Lexical resource:*** Do you use a wide range of vocabulary accurately and appropriately? Do you spell correctly?

4. ***Grammatical range and accuracy:*** Do you use many different sentence structures or do you always use the same ones? How often do you make mistakes with your grammar?

考生可能会对拿到的分数感到疑惑，如果拿到6分代表什么?阅卷者是以什么标准评分的呢?下面是由英国文化协会、澳大利亚教育国际开发署以及剑桥大学考试委员会所提供的评分标准。

表格中，对于每个分数的界定或许不是很清楚（对母语为英语的人来说亦然），但考生要谨记，阅卷者主要会以下面4点作为评分的依据：

1. 完成任务情况

2. 连贯与衔接

3. 词汇资源

4. 语法结构的范围和准确性

（表格资料来源：www.ielts.org）

Band（得分）	Task Achievement 完成任务情况
9分	• fully satisfies all the requirements of the task • clearly presents a fully developed response
8分	• covers all requirements of the task sufficiently • presents, highlights and illustrates key features/bullet points clearly and appropriately
7分	• covers the requirements of the task • (Academic) presents a clear overview of main trends, differences or stages • (General Training) presents a clear purpose, with the tone consistent and appropriate • clearly presents and highlights key features/bullet points but could be more fully extended
6分	• addresses the requirements of the task • (Academic) presents an overview with information appropriately selected • (General Training) presents a purpose that is generally clear; there may be inconsistencies in tone • presents and adequately highlights key features/bullet points but details may be irrelevant, inappropriate or inaccurate
5分	• generally addresses the task; the format may be inappropriate in places • (Academic) recounts detail mechanically with no clear overview; there may be no data to support the description • (General Training) may present a purpose for the letter that is unclear at times; the tone may be variable and sometimes inappropriate • presents, but inadequately covers, key features/bullet points; there may be a tendency to focus on details

4分	• attempts to address the task but does not cover all key features/bullet points; the format may be inappropriate • (General Training) fails to clearly explain the purpose of the letter; the tone may be inappropriate • may confuse key features/bullet points with detail; parts may be unclear, irrelevant, repetitive or inaccurate
3分	• fails to address the task, which may have been completely misunderstood • presents limited ideas which may be largely irrelevant/repetitive
2分	• answer is barely related to the task
1分	• answer is completely unrelated to the task
0分	• does not attend • does not attempt the task in any way • writes a totally memorised response

Band (得分)	Coherence and Cohesion 连贯与衔接
9分	• uses cohesion in such a way that it attracts no attention • skilfully manages paragraphing
8分	• sequences information and ideas logically • manages all aspects of cohesion well • uses paragraphing sufficiently and appropriately
7分	• logically organises information and ideas; there is a clear progression throughout • uses a range of cohesive devices appropriately although there may be some under/overuse
6分	• arranges information and ideas coherently and there is a clear overall progression • uses cohesive devices effectively, but cohesion within and/or between sentences may be faulty or mechanical • may not always use referencing clearly or appropriately
5分	• presents information with some organisation but there may be a lack of overall progression • makes inadequate, inaccurate or over-use of cohesive devices • may be repetitive because of lack of referencing and substitution
4分	• presents information and ideas but these are not arranged coherently and there is no clear progression in the response • uses some basic cohesive devices but these may be inaccurate or repetitive
3分	• does not organise ideas logically • may use a very limited range of cohesive devices, and those used may not indicate a logical relationship between ideas

2分	• has very little control of organisational features
1分	• fails to communicate any message
0分	• does not attend • does not attempt the task in any way • writes a totally memorised response

Band (得分)	Lexical Resource 词汇资源
9分	• uses a wide range of vocabulary with very natural and sophisticated control of lexical features; rare minor errors occur only as "slips"
8分	• uses a wide range of vocabulary fluently and flexibly to convey precise meanings • skilfully uses uncommon lexical items but there may be occasional inaccuracies in word choice and collocation • produces rare errors in spelling and/or word formation
7分	• uses a sufficient range of vocabulary to allow some flexibility and precision • uses less common lexical items with some awareness of style and collocation • may produce occasional errors in word choice, spelling and/or word formation
6分	• uses an adequate range of vocabulary for the task • attempts to use less common vocabulary but with some inaccuracy • makes some errors in spelling and/or word formation, but they do not impede communication
5分	• uses a limited range of vocabulary, but this is minimally adequate for the task • may make noticeable errors in spelling and/or word formation that may cause some difficulty for the reader
4分	• uses only basic vocabulary which may be used repetitively or which may be inappropriate for the task • has limited control of word formation and/or spelling • errors may cause strain for the reader

3分	• uses only a very limited range of words and expressions with very limited control of word formation and/or spelling • errors may severely distort the message
2分	• uses an extremely limited range of vocabulary; essentially no control of word formation and/or spelling
1分	• can only use a few isolated words
0分	• does not attend • does not attempt the task in any way • writes a totally memorised response

Band (得分)	Grammatical Range and Accuracy 语法结构的范围和准确性
9分	• uses a wide range of structures with full flexibility and accuracy; rare minor errors occur only as "slips"
8分	• uses a wide range of structures • the majority of sentences are error-free • makes only very occasional errors or inappropriacies
7分	• uses a variety of complex structures • produces frequent error-free sentences • has good control of grammar and punctuation but may make a few errors
6分	• uses a mix of simple and complex sentence forms • makes some errors in grammar and punctuation but they rarely reduce communication
5分	• uses only a limited range of structures • attempts complex sentences but these tend to be less accurate than simple sentences • may make frequent grammatical errors and punctuation may be faulty; errors can cause some difficulty for the reader
4分	• uses only a very limited range of structures with only rare use of subordinate clauses • some structures are accurate but errors predominate, and punctuation is often faulty
3分	• attempts sentence forms but errors in grammar and punctuation predominate and distort meaning
2分	• cannot use sentence forms except in memorised phrases

1分	• cannot use sentence forms at all
0分	• does not attend • does not attempt the task in any way • writes a totally memorised response

IELTS Writing Task 2 Band Descriptors

IELTS 写作TASK 2 评分标准

Band (得分)	Task Achievement 完成任务情况
9分	• fully addresses all parts of the task • presents a fully developed position in answer to the question with relevant, fully extended and well supported ideas
8分	• sufficiently addresses all parts of the task • presents a well developed response to the question with relevant, extended and supported ideas
7分	• addresses all parts of the task • presents a clear position throughout the response • presents, extends and supports main ideas, but there may be a tendency to overgeneralise and/or supporting ideas may lack focus
6分	• addresses all parts of the task although some parts may be more fully covered than others • presents a relevant position although the conclusions may become unclear or repetitive • presents relevant main ideas but some may be inadequately developed/unclear
5分	• addresses the task only partially; the format may be inappropriate in places • expresses a position but the development is not always clear and there may be no conclusions drawn • presents some main ideas but these are limited and not sufficiently developed; there maybe irrelevant detail
4分	• responds to the task only in a minimal way or the answer is tangential; the format may be inappropriate • presents a position but this is unclear • presents some main ideas but these are difficult to identify and maybe repetitive, irrelevant or not well supported

3分	• does not adequately address any part of the task • does not express a clear position • presents few ideas, which are largely undeveloped or irrelevant
2分	• barely responds to the task • does not express a position • may attempt to present one or two ideas but there is no development
1分	• answer is completely unrelated to the task
0分	• does not attend • does not attempt the task in any way • writes a totally memorised response

Band （得分）	Coherence and Cohesion 连贯与衔接
9分	• uses cohesion in such a way that it attracts no attention • skilfully manages paragraphing
8分	• sequences information and ideas logically • manages all aspects of cohesion well • uses paragraphing sufficiently and appropriately
7分	• logically organises information and ideas; there is a clear progression throughout • uses a range of cohesive devices appropriately although there may be some under/overuse • presents a clear central topic within each paragraph
6分	• arranges information and ideas coherently and there is a clear overall progression • uses cohesive devices effectively, but cohesion within and/or between sentences may be faulty or mechanical • may not always use referencing clearly or appropriately • uses paragraphing, but not always logically
5分	• presents information with some organisation but there may be a lack of overall progression • makes inadequate, inaccurate or overuse of cohesive devices • may be repetitive because of lack of referencing and substitution • may not write in paragraphs, or paragraphing may be inadequate
4分	• presents information and ideas but these are not arranged coherently and there is no clear progression in the response • uses some basic cohesive devices but these may be inaccurate or repetitive • may not write in paragraphs or their use may be confusing

3分	• does not organise ideas logically • may use a very limited range of cohesive devices, and those used may not indicate a logical relationship between ideas
2分	• has very little control of organisational features
1分	• fails to communicate any message
0分	• does not attend • does not attempt the task in any way • writes a totally memorised response

Band (得分)	Lexical Resource 词汇资源
9分	• uses a wide range of vocabulary with very natural and sophisticated control of lexical features; rare minor errors occur only as "slips"
8分	• uses a wide range of vocabulary fluently and flexibly to convey precise meanings • skilfully uses uncommon lexical items but there may be occasional inaccuracies in word choice and collocation • produces rare errors in spelling and/or word formation
7分	• uses a sufficient range of vocabulary to allow some flexibility and precision • uses less common lexical items with some awareness of style and collocation • may produce occasional errors in word choice, spelling and/or word formation
6分	• uses an adequate range of vocabulary for the task • attempts to use less common vocabulary but with some inaccuracy • makes some errors in spelling and/or word formation, but they do not impede communication
5分	• uses a limited range of vocabulary, but this is minimally adequate for the task • may make noticeable errors in spelling and/or word formation that may cause some difficulty for the reader
4分	• uses only basic vocabulary which may be used repetitively or which may be inappropriate for the task. • has limited control of word formation and/or spelling; errors may cause strain for the reader

3分	• uses only a very limited range of words and expressions with very limited control of word formation and/or spelling • errors may severely distort the message
2分	• uses an extremely limited range of vocabulary; essentially no control of word formation and/or spelling
1分	• can only use a few isolated words
0分	• does not attend • does not attempt the task in any way • writes a totally memorised response

Band （得分）	Grammatical Range and Accuracy 语法结构的范围和准确性
9分	• uses a wide range of structures with full flexibility and accuracy; rare minor errors occur only as "slips"
8分	• uses a wide range of structures • the majority of sentences are error-free • makes only very occasional errors or inappropriacies
7分	• uses a variety of complex structures • produces frequent error-free sentences • has good control of grammar and punctuation but may make a few errors
6分	• uses a mix of simple and complex sentence forms • makes some errors in grammar and punctuation but they rarely reduce communication
5分	• uses only a limited range of structures • attempts complex sentences but these tend to be less accurate than simple sentences • may make frequent grammatical errors and punctuation may be faulty; errors can cause some difficulty for the reader
4分	• uses only a very limited range of structures with only rare use of subordinate clauses • some structures are accurate but errors predominate, and punctuation is often faulty
3分	• attempts sentence forms but errors in grammar and punctuation predominate and distort meaning
2分	• cannot use sentence forms except in memorised phrases

1分	• cannot use sentence forms at all
0分	• does not attend • does not attempt the task in any way • writes a totally memorised response

IELTS

WRITE RIGHT

学术类写作 TASK 1

Writing Task 1: Academic Module

Question Types

One particularly challenging aspect of Academic Writing Task 1 is the range of different question types used (see below). Although this may seem daunting at first, it is important to remember that the same data can be presented in many different ways and that two very different graphs or diagrams can often demonstrate exactly the same thing. For instance, line graphs are often very similar to column graphs. It is, therefore, often possible to use exactly the same sentence structures and vocabulary to describe them. A wide range of different question types have been included in the following pages in order to highlight the similarities and differences in the language needed to describe each of the various question types that you may face. Note that the words "***graph***" and "***chart***" are used interchangeably and that the word "***figure***" is used to refer to any graph, chart or diagram.

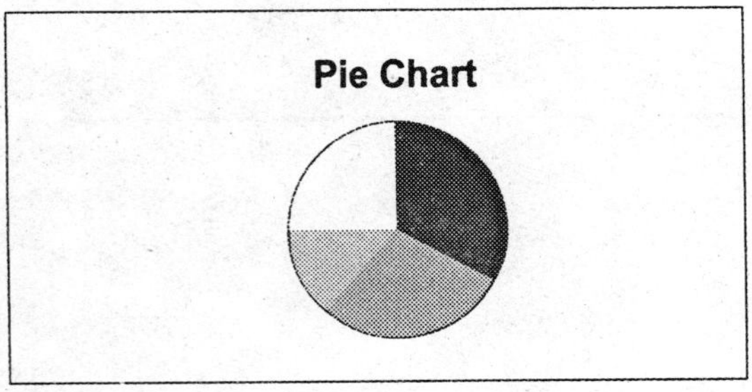

(饼状图)

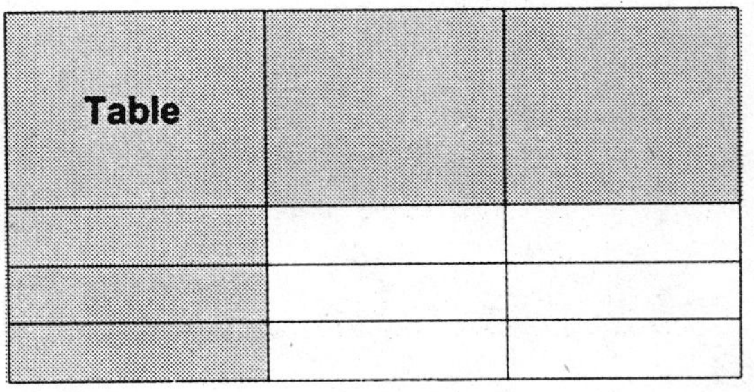

(表格)

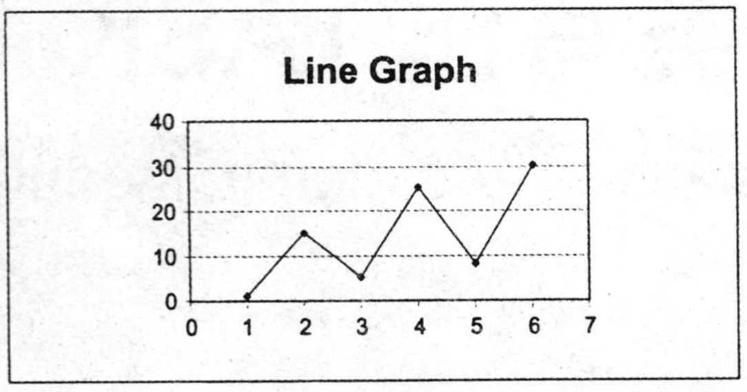

(曲线图)

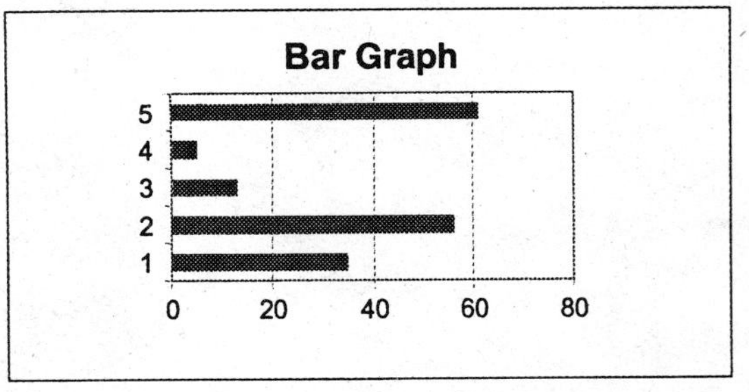

(条状图)

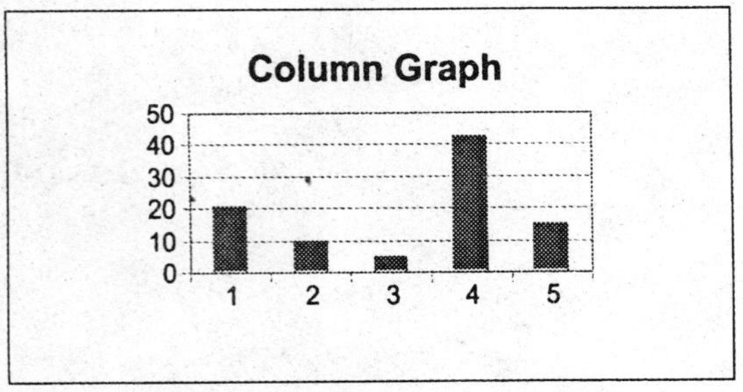

(柱状图)

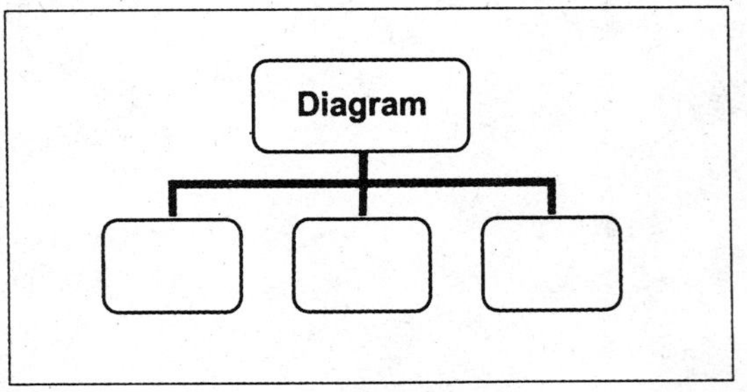

(流程图)

Line Graph
曲线图

Question 1 Birth Rates in China and the USA
中国与美国的出生率

WRITING TASK 1

You should spend about 20 minutes on this task.

The graph below compares changes in the birth rates of China and the USA between 1920 and 2000.

Summarise the information by selecting and reporting the main features, and make comparisons where relevant.

Write at least 150 words.

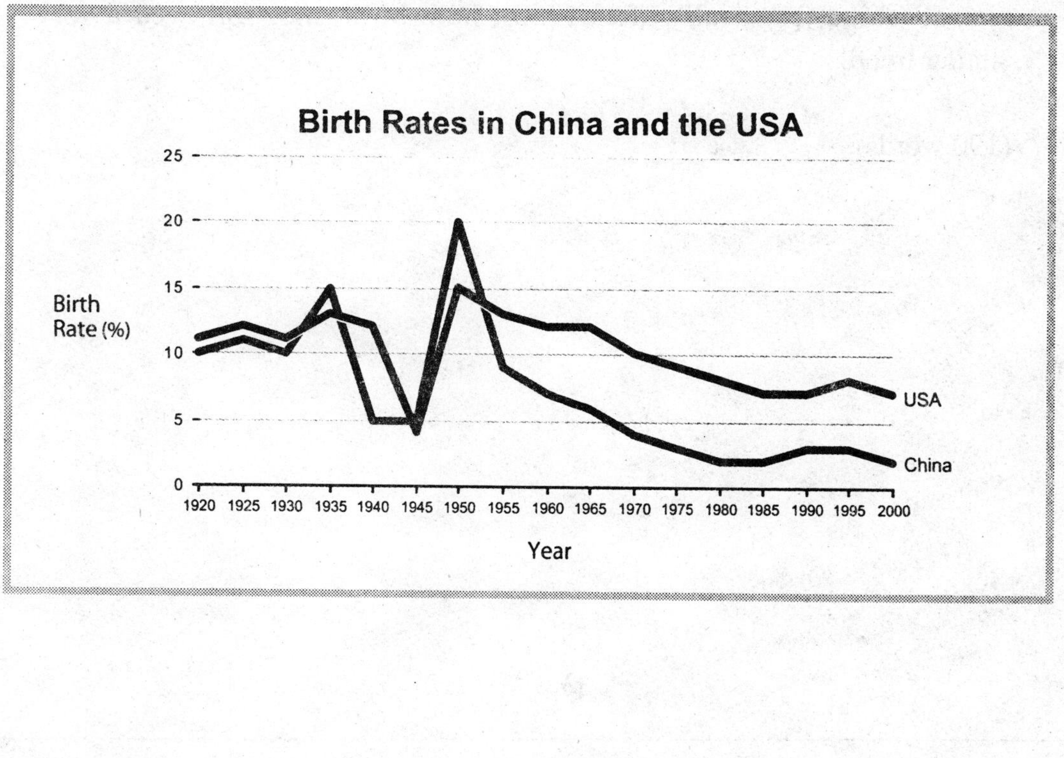

Model Answer A: IELTS Band 5^+

The figure given shows the birth rates of China and the USA between 1920 and 2000. Clearly, both rates fluctuated dramatically during this period.

China's birth rate rose from around 10 percent in the 1920s to 15 percent in 1935. Then it fell sharply to around 5 percent in both 1940 and 1945. It increased rapidly to a peak of 20 percent in 1950. After this it fell dramatically to less than 10 percent in 1955. Finally, it decreased steadily to about 2 percent in 1980 and remained at this level until 2000.

Meanwhile, the US birth rate fluctuated at around 12 percent from 1920 to 1940. It decreased dramatically to under 5 percent in 1945. Next it increased rapidly to a peak of about 15 percent in 1950. After 1950, it fell gradually to about 12 percent in the 1960s and around 7 or 8 percent during the last 20 years of this period.

Therefore, although the US birth rate was generally higher than the birth rate of China (especially after 1950), both birth rates followed a very similar trend.

(190 words)

Model Answer B: IELTS Band 7+

A glance at the graph provided reveals some striking similarities between the Chinese and US birth rates during the period from 1920 to 2000. It is evident that both nations saw considerable fluctuations in fertility, with lows during the 1940s and highs during the 1950s.

Increasing from approximately 10 percent in 1920 to 15 percent in 1935, China's birth rate then plunged to a low of just 5 percent in the 1940s. This was followed by a period of exponential growth, with fertility in the country reaching a peak of 20 percent in 1950. The latter half of the century, however, brought a sustained decline in this figure.

The US birth rate, meanwhile, fluctuated at somewhere between 11 and 13 percent prior to 1940, before dropping sharply to less than 5 percent in 1945. The following 5 years saw a rapid climb in this rate, to somewhere in the vicinity of 15 percent in 1950, followed by a steady fall.

It is interesting to note that while the birth rates of both countries were comparable until 1950, the gap between the two widened after this time as fertility in China slid away.

(207 words)

Model Sentence Structures 句型示范

Sentence 1	**IELTS 5**	The graph shows some similarities between the birth rates of China and the USA from 1920 to 2000.
	IELTS 6	The graph provided reveals some surprising similarities between the Chinese and US birth rates during the period from 1920 to 2000.
	IELTS 7+	A glance at the graph provided reveals some striking similarities between the Chinese and US birth rates during the period from 1920 to 2000.
Sentence 2	**IELTS 5**	Clearly, the birth rates of both countries fluctuated dramatically, with lows in the 1940s and highs in the 1950s.
	IELTS 6	It is evident that the fertility rates of both nations fluctuated considerably, with lows during the 1940s and highs during the 1950s.
	IELTS 7+	It is evident that both nations saw considerable fluctuations in fertility, with lows during the 1940s and highs during the 1950s.
Sentence 3	**IELTS 5**	First, China's birth rate increased from about 10 percent in 1920 to 15 percent in 1935. Then it decreased sharply to just 5 percent in the 1940s.
	IELTS 6	China's birth rate first increased from approximately 10 percent in 1920 to 15 percent in 1935, then plunged to a low of just 5 percent in the 1940s.
	IELTS 7+	Increasing from approximately 10 percent in 1920 to 15 percent in 1935, China's birth rate then plunged to a low of just 5 percent in the 1940s.

Sentence 4	IELTS 5	Then the US birth rate increased markedly to over 15 percent in 1950.
	IELTS 6	There was then a marked increase in US fertility to over 15 percent in 1950.
	IELTS 7^+	The US then saw a marked increase to over 15 percent in 1950.

Academic Vocabulary 高分词汇

Basic 基础 5⁺分	Intermediate 中级 6⁺分	Advanced 高级 7⁺分
show (v.)		reveal (v.)
increase (v.)	rise (v.) climb (v.) grow (v.)	
increase (n.)	rise (n.) growth (n.)	
decrease (v./n.)	fall (v./n.) drop (v./n.)	decline (v./n.)
sharp (adj.)	dramatic (adj.)	rapid (adj.) considerable (adj.) exponential (adj.) marked (adj.)
sharply (adv.)	dramatically (adv.)	rapidly (adv.) considerably (adv.) exponentially (adv.) markedly (adv.)
fall sharply	decrease dramatically	slide away plunge (v.)
	gradual (adj.)	steady (adj.)
	gradually (adv.)	steadily (adv.)
	birth rate	fertility (n.)
about (adv.)		approximately (adv.) somewhere in the vicinity of

Test Your Comprehension 综合练习

Answer these questions by circling A, B or C

1. Which of these is the best way to start your essay?
   A. The graph shows...
   B. A glance at the graph provided reveals...
   C. The figure given shows...

2. What is the past tense form of "*rise*"?
   A. rose
   B. rised
   C. rising

3. What verb tense(s) does the writer use in these two essays?
   A. present tense
   B. past tense
   C. present and past tense

Answer these questions by writing YES or NO

4. In paragraph 3 of Model Answer B, "*climb*" is a verb.

5. In both of these essays the word "*peak*" is a verb which means "*low point*".

6. The sentence structures used in Model Answer A are too repetitive.

7. Model Answer B is too long.

8. The US and Chinese birth rates remained relatively stable between 1920 and 2000.

Check your answers

1. **B**

"***The graph shows***" is not the best way to start your essay because many other candidates will write exactly the same thing. If you want a higher score than other candidates you should try to be different from them.

2. **A**

3. **C**

The writer mostly uses past tense in these model answers because the years on the graph are in the past (1920-2000). However, present tense is used in sentences starting with "***the graph***" because the graph is here, now. So you can write, "***The graph shows that the Chinese birth rate increased***".

4. **NO**

"***Climb***" is often a verb. However, in paragraph 3 of Model Answer B, it is used as a noun. So you could write, "***The birth rate climbed***" or "***There was a climb in the birth rate***". Both are acceptable.

5. **NO**

"***Peak***" means "***high point***" and is a noun in both of these model answers. It can also be used as a verb, so you could actually write, "***The birth rate reached a peak***" or "***The birth rate peaked***".

6. **YES**

Model Answer A uses the same sentence structure several times. Two examples of this structure are, "***It fell sharply***" and "***It increased rapidly***". Model Answer B is better.

7. **NO**

Remember that 150 words is a minimum word limit—there is no maximum word limit. After you pass 150 words, time is more important than the number of words you write. Do not work on Writing Task 1 for more than 20 minutes.

8. **NO**

The birth rates of both countries fluctuated.

Line Graph and Pie Chart

曲线图与饼状图

Question 2 Crime in the UK

英国的犯罪率

WRITING TASK 1

You should spend about 20 minutes on this task.

> ***The two figures below show the rate of criminal convictions among men and women of different ages in the UK and the proportion of male and female prison inmates in the British prison system.***
>
> ***Summarise the information by selecting and reporting the main features, and make comparisons where relevant.***

Write at least 150 words.

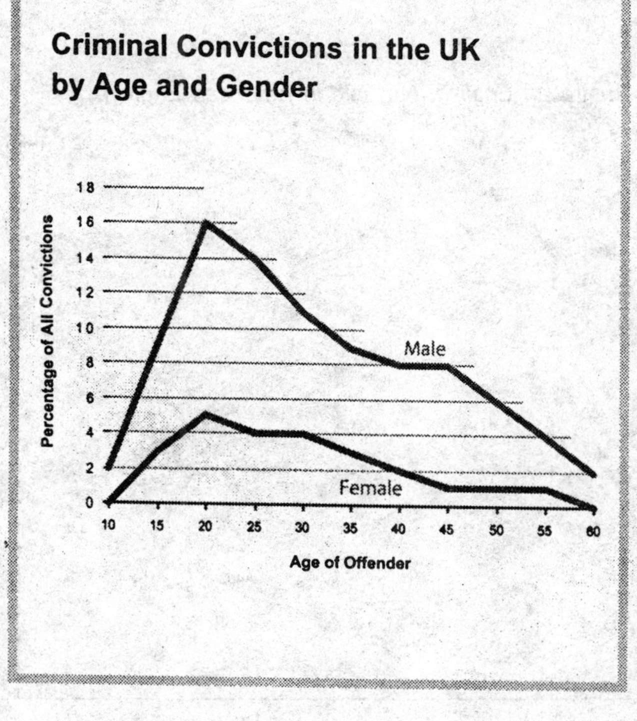

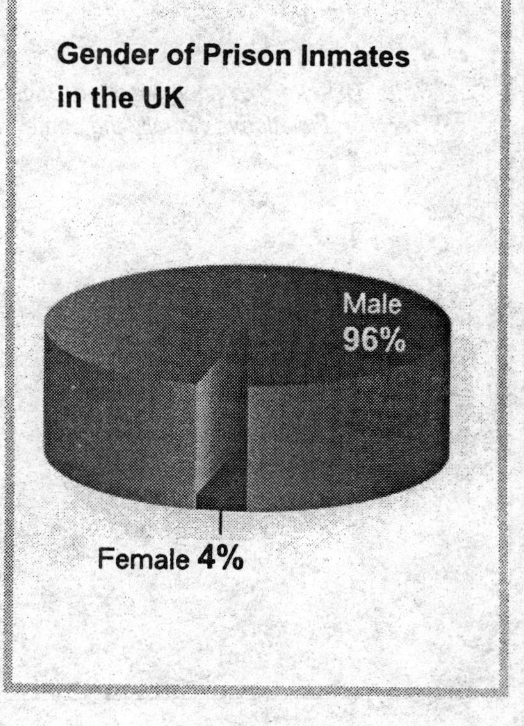

5+分

Model Answer A: IELTS Band 5⁺

The first figure shows the percentage of criminal convictions in the UK that occur among men and women of different ages, while the second compares the percentage of male and female prisoners in British *gaols.

It is clear from the graphs that most convicted criminals in the UK are in their early twenties and that men are much more likely to be convicted than women. The male conviction rate increases sharply from just 2 percent among 10-year-olds to about 16 percent among 20-year-olds. Meanwhile, the rate of convictions among females rises from 0 percent at the age of 10 to around 5 percent at 20. After this, the percentage of criminal convictions for both men and women decreases. According to the figures, 60-year-old men only commit about 2 percent of all crimes and 60-year-old women do not commit any crimes at all.

Not surprisingly, the second graph shows that 96 percent of all prisoners are men while only 4 percent are female.

(162 words)

Note: This word is spelt "gaol" in British/Australian English, but "jail" in American English. The pronunciation is virtually the same.

Model Answer B: IELTS Band 7⁺

Given are two figures concerning criminality in Britain. The first provides data on the rates of conviction among men and women of various ages, while the second indicates the gender balance of the UK prison population.

It is apparent from the information supplied that the rate of conviction among Brits of both sexes increases exponentially during adolescence and peaks at the age of about 20. Also evident is the fact that men are far more likely to offend than women. From a negligible 2 percent among 10-year-old boys, the male conviction rate soars to approximately 16 percent among 20-year-olds. The percentage of female offenders, meanwhile, climbs from 0 percent among girls of 10 to some 5 percent for 20-year-olds. The subsequent decades, however, see dramatic decreases in criminality among both sexes. A mere 2 percent of crimes are committed by 60-year-old men and 0 percent by women of the same age.

As for the proportion of male and female prison inmates, men outnumber women 24 to 1. Some 96 percent of all prisoners are men, while the remainder are female.

(180 words)

Model Sentence Structures 句型示范

Sentence 1	IELTS 5	These two figures are about crime in Britain.
	IELTS 6	The two figures given concern criminality in Britain.
	IELTS 7+	Given are two figures concerning criminality in Britain.
Sentence 2	IELTS 5	The rate of conviction among males increases sharply from just 2 percent among 10-year-old boys to about 16 percent among 20-year-olds.
	IELTS 6	The male conviction rate soars from a negligible 2 percent among 10-year-old boys to about 16 percent among 20-year-olds.
	IELTS 7+	From a negligible 2 percent among 10-year-old boys, the male conviction rate soars to approximately 16 percent among 20-year-olds.
Sentence 3	IELTS 5	However, crime decreases dramatically among men and women over the following 20 or 30 years.
	IELTS 6	However, there are dramatic decreases in criminal convictions among both sexes over the subsequent decades.
	IELTS 7+	The subsequent decades, however, see dramatic decreases in criminality among both sexes.

Sentence 4	IELTS 5	Clearly, the rate of conviction among British men and women increases sharply during the teenage years and reaches a peak when they are about 20 years old.
	IELTS 6	It is clear from the information given that the rate of conviction among British people of both sexes increases exponentially during adolescence and peaks at the age of about 20.
	IELTS 7+	It is apparent from the information supplied that the rate of conviction among Brits of both sexes increases exponentially during adolescence and peaks at the age of about 20.

Academic Vocabulary 高分词汇

Basic 基础 5	Intermediate 中级 6	Advanced 高级 7
gaol (n.)	prison (n.)	
increase (v.)	climb (v.) rise (v.)	
sharp (adj.)	dramatic (adj.)	exponential (adj.)
sharply (adv.)	dramatically (adv.)	exponentially (adv.)
	increase dramatically	increase exponentially soar (v.)
just (adv.)	only (adv.)	a negligible/ a mere
about (adv.) around (adv.)	some (adv.)	approximately (adv.)
	prisoner (n.)	offender (n.) convicted criminal/ prison inmate
about (prep.)	on (prep.)	concerning (prep.)
clear (adj.)		apparent (adj.) evident (adj.)

Test Your Comprehension 综合练习

Answer these questions by circling A, B or C

1. What verb tense(s) does the writer use in these two essays?
   A. future tense
   B. present and past tense
   C. present tense

2. Which of these sentences is wrong?
   A. 96 percentage of people in gaol are men.
   B. A large percentage of people in gaol are men.
   C. 96 percent of people in gaol are men.

3. Which of these phrases is a bad way to start your essay?
   A. Given are two figures concerning...
   B. A glance at the two figures provided reveals...
   C. These two figures show...

4. Which age group has the highest incidence of criminality in Britain?
   A. the aged
   B. children
   C. adolescents

5. In Model Answer B, the word "***subsequent***" means:
   A. later
   B. earlier
   C. at the same time

Answer these questions by writing YES or NO

6. In Model Answer B, the word "***peak***" is used as a noun.

7. In Model Answer B, the phrase "***men outnumber women 24 to 1***" means that there are more women than men.

8. In the phrase "***data on the rates of conviction***" (see Model Answer B), the word "***on***" means "***about***".

9. "***Occur***" (see Model Answer A) is a more formal, and better, way to say "***happen***".

Check your answers

1. **C**

   The writer uses present tense because the question does not mention any year.

2. **A**

   The word "***percent***" must be used with a number, while the word "***percentage***" can only be used with adjectives like "***high***" or "***low***". Thus, you could write, "***80 percent of people in France can speak English***" or "***A high percentage of people in France can speak English***".

3. **C**

   "***These two figures show***" is not a good way to start because it is too simple. It is also exactly what every IELTS text book and every other IELTS student writes. Be different!

4. **C**

   There is more crime among teenagers than any other group.

5. **A**

6. **NO**

   In this case, it is a verb. Remember that "***peak***" can be a verb or a noun.

7. **NO**

   In fact, it means that there are more men than women.

8. **YES**

   "***On***" sometimes means "***about***". For example, you might write, "***I am reading a book on endangered animals***".

9. **YES**

   "***Happen***" is often used in spoken English, while "***occur***" and "***take place***" are used in formal English, especially writing.

Pie Chart

饼状图

Question 3 Leisure Activities in Europe

欧洲的休闲生活

WRITING TASK 1

You should spend about 20 minutes on this task.

The following two pie charts show the results of a survey into the popularity of various leisure activities among European adults in 1985 and 1995.

Summarise the information by selecting and reporting the main features, and make comparisons where relevant.

Write at least 150 words.

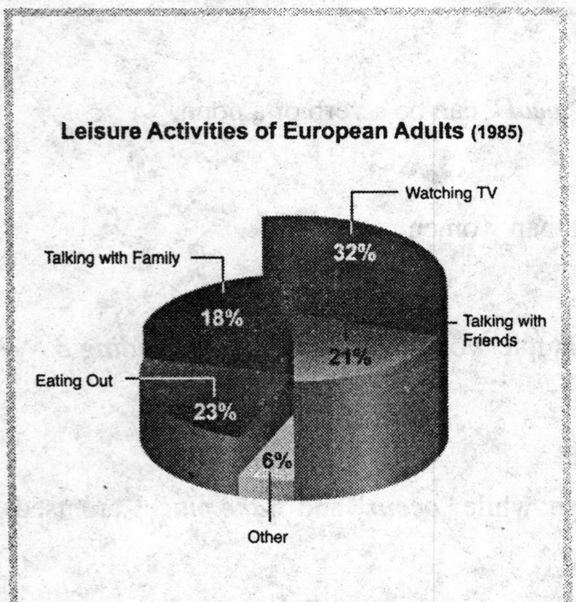

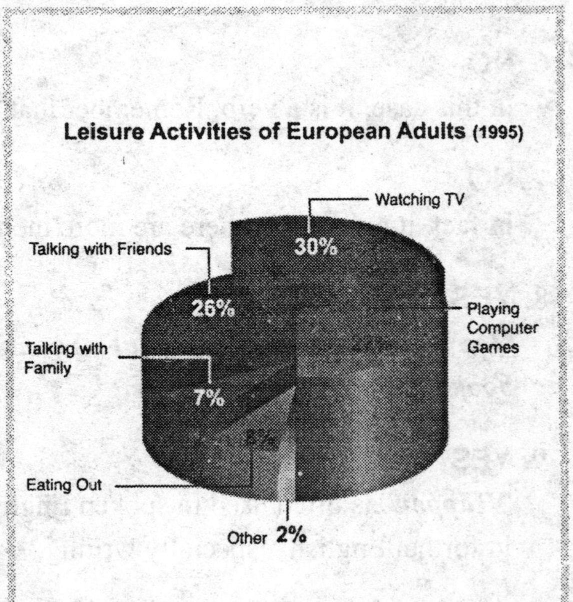

Model Answer A: IELTS Band 5⁺

The two pie charts given show the popularity of several different hobbies among European adults in 1985 and 1995.

Clearly, watching television was the number one leisure activity in both years, at 32 percent in 1985 and 30 percent in 1995. However, the most obvious change to occur during this time was that computer games became much more popular. In 1985, nobody said that playing computer games was their favourite leisure activity, but in 1995 some 27 percent of European adults named this as the activity that they enjoyed the most. The only other hobby that became more popular was talking with friends, which rose from 21 percent in 1985 to 26 percent in 1995.

By contrast, all other activities became less popular. For instance, while 23 percent of European adults named eating out as their favourite leisure activity in 1985, this figure was just 8 percent in 1995. Similarly, the percentage of people who said that they liked talking with family, other activities or watching TV also decreased.

(169 words)

Model Answer B: IELTS Band 7^+

A glance at the two pie charts provided reveals the relative popularity of various leisure activities among European adults in 1985 and 1995.

Of these activities, watching television was the most widely enjoyed in both years, at 32 percent in 1985 and a slightly lower 30 percent in 1995. Yet, by far the most significant change to take place during this period was the increased popularity of computer games. Not a single respondent to the survey rated playing computer games as their preferred leisure activity in 1985. However, by 1995 this figure stood at 27 percent—the second highest overall. Also more popular in 1995 was talking with friends, at 26 percent compared to 21 percent a decade earlier.

In stark contrast, however, all other activities decreased in popularity. Eating out—which was the second most widely enjoyed pastime in 1985, accounting for 23 percent of respondents—slipped to a mere 8 percent in 1995. Likewise, there were also considerable decreases in the popularity ratings of talking with family, other activities and (as previously mentioned) watching television.

(177 words)

Model Sentence Structures 句型示范

Sentence 1	IELTS 5	None of the people who were surveyed said that playing computer games was their favourite leisure activity in 1985.
	IELTS 6	None of the respondents to the survey named playing computer games as their preferred leisure activity in 1985.
	IELTS 7⁺	Not a single respondent to the survey rated playing computer games as their preferred leisure activity in 1985.
Sentence 2	IELTS 5	Talking with friends was more popular in 1995 too, at 26 percent compared to 21 percent 10 years before.
	IELTS 6	Talking with friends was also more popular in 1995, at 26 percent compared to 21 percent a decade earlier.
	IELTS 7⁺	Also more popular in 1995 was talking with friends, at 26 percent compared to 21 percent a decade earlier.
Sentence 3	IELTS 5	On the other hand, all other activities became less popular.
	IELTS 6	In stark contrast, however, the popularity of all other activities decreased.
	IELTS 7⁺	In stark contrast, however, all other activities decreased in popularity.

Sentence 4	IELTS 5	Eating out was the second most popular hobby in 1985, at 23 percent of all people surveyed. However, it fell to just 8 percent in 1995.
	IELTS 6	Eating out was the second most widely enjoyed pastime in 1985, accounting for 23 percent of respondents. However, it slipped to a mere 8 percent in 1995.
	IELTS 7+	Eating out—which was the second most widely enjoyed pastime in 1985, accounting for 23 percent of respondents—slipped to a mere 8 percent in 1995.

Academic Vocabulary 高分词汇

Basic 基础 5+分	Intermediate 中级 6分	Advanced 高级 7+分
decrease (n./v.)		slip (v.)
just (adv.) only (adv.)		a mere
several different	various (adj.)	
hobby (n.)		pastime (n.) leisure activity
popular (adj.)		widely enjoyed
*favourite (adj.)	preferred (adj.)	
	likewise (adv.) similarly (adv.)	
	however (adv.)	yet (adv.)
	by contrast	in stark contrast, however, ...

Note: This word is spelt "favourite" in British/Australian English, but "favorite" in American English. Some other words that follow this rule are "neighbour/neighbor", "flavour/flavor", "colour/color" and "honour/honor".

Test Your Comprehension 综合练习

Answer these questions by circling A, B or C

1. Which was the least popular leisure activity in 1985?
   A. other
   B. talking with family
   C. watching TV

2. "***Popular***" is an adjective. The noun is:
   A. popularity
   B. popularness
   C. population

3. In Model Answer B, the word "***likewise***" means:
   A. similarly
   B. such as
   C. enjoy

4. Which is the most formal?
   A. as previously mentioned
   B. like I said before
   C. as I mentioned before

Answer these questions by writing YES or NO

5. "***For instance***" (see Model Answer A) means "***for example***", but is slightly better because it sounds a little more formal and fewer candidates use it.

6. "***Respondents***" (see Model Answer B) are people who ask questions, carry out surveys and make charts/graphs.

7. "***Not a single respondent to the survey rated playing computer games as their preferred leisure activity in 1985***" (see Model Answer B) means that very few people said they liked playing computer games in 1985.

8. The writer uses the word "***similarly***" (see Model Answer A) to connect "***eating out in restaurants***" and "***chatting with friends***" because both of these leisure activities became less popular.

Check your answers

1. **A**

   Remember that "***least***" is the opposite of "***most***".

2. **A**

   When you learn vocabulary, try to learn all the different forms of a word.

3. **A**

   Do not forget that the word "***like***" can mean "***enjoy***" or "***similar to***".

4. **A**

   "***As previously mentioned***" is a good way to say "***like I said before***" in academic writing.

5. **YES**

   Try to be different.

6. **NO**

   "***Respondents***" are people who answer questions in a survey. You can also say "***respondents to the survey***".

7. **NO**

   "***Not a single respondent***" means "***nobody***".

8. **YES**

   "***Similarly***" is always used to connect facts which are the same or similar.

Table and Pie Chart
表格与饼状图

Question 4 Internet Use in Europe
欧洲的网络使用

WRITING TASK 1

You should spend about 20 minutes on this task.

The figures below compare the number of internet users in several European nations as well as the prevalence of online shopping in these countries.

Summarise the information by selecting and reporting the main features, and make comparisons where relevant.

Write at least 150 words.

Total Number of Internet Users (in millions)

COUNTRY	1995	2000	2004
Switzerland	1	2	4
Germany	5	14	15
France	2	3	6
Spain	0.5	0.7	2
UK	16	22	41

Internet Shopping in Europe (2004)

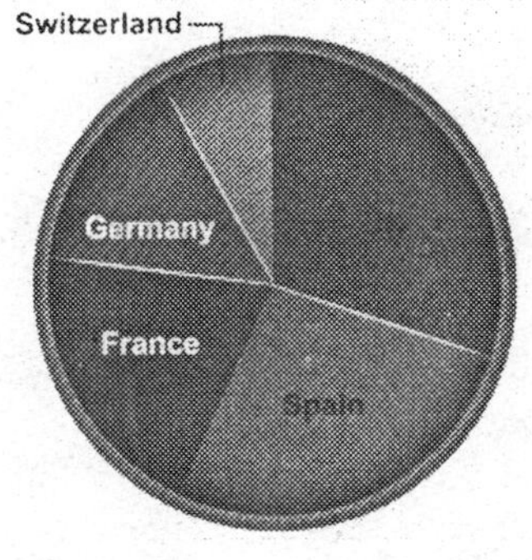

Model Answer A: IELTS Band 5⁺

The first figure compares the number of people connected to the Internet in five European countries in 1995, 2000 and 2004, while the second shows the level of internet shopping in these countries in 2004.

Clearly, Britain had the most internet users. The number of British people using the Internet increased dramatically from 16 million in 1995 to 22 million in 2000 and then 41 million in 2004. Germany was second. The number of internet users in this country rose from 5 million in 1995 to 14 million in 2000 and then 15 million in 2004. France had the third most users during this time, with 2 million in 1995, 3 million in 2000 and 6 million in 2004. Meanwhile, the countries with the fewest internet users were Switzerland and Spain.

Interestingly, Britain also had the highest level of internet shopping in 2004. It had twice as much online shopping as Germany and three times as much as Switzerland. Meanwhile, the levels of internet shopping in France and Spain were slightly lower than that of the UK.

(177 words)

Model Answer B: IELTS Band 7⁺

Given are two figures providing a comparison of internet use in five European countries (namely Switzerland, Germany, France, Spain and the UK) in 1995, 2000 and 2004, as well as the popularity of internet shopping in these countries.

It is evident from the information provided that Britain had by far the highest number of internet users in all three years. From 16 million in 1995, the number of British users climbed steadily to 22 million in 2000, before soaring to a staggering 41 million in 2004. Second in terms of internet use was Germany. This country saw a threefold increase during the period in question, from 5 million people in 1995 to 14 million in 2000 and 15 million in 2004. A similar increase took place in France. The two nations with the fewest internet users, meanwhile, were Switzerland and Spain.

It is also interesting to note that internet shopping was far more common in the UK than in any other country listed. In fact, the prevalence of internet shopping in Britain was double that of Germany and triple that of Switzerland. France and Spain, meanwhile, had moderate levels of online shopping.

(192 words)

Model Sentence Structures 句型示范

Sentence 1	IELTS 5	Germany was second when it came to internet use.
	IELTS 6	Germany was second in terms of internet use.
	IELTS 7+	Second in terms of internet use was Germany.
Sentence 2	IELTS 5	The number of internet users in this country increased threefold during this time.
	IELTS 6	There was a threefold increase in the number of internet users in this country during the period in question.
	IELTS 7+	This country saw a threefold increase during the period in question.
Sentence 3	IELTS 5	There was a similar increase in France.
	IELTS 6	France saw a similar increase.
	IELTS 7+	A similar increase took place in France.
Sentence 4	IELTS 5	Actually, internet shopping was two times as popular in Britain as it was in Germany and three times more popular than in Switzerland.
	IELTS 6	In fact, internet shopping was twice as prevalent in Britain as it was in Germany and three times more prevalent than in Switzerland.
	IELTS 7+	In fact, the prevalence of internet shopping in Britain was double that of Germany and triple that of Switzerland.

Academic Vocabulary 高分词汇

Basic 基础 5+	Intermediate 中级 6+	Advanced 高级 7+
	compare (v.)	provide a comparison of
level (n.)		popularity (n.) prevalence (n.)
increase (n./v.)	rise (n./v.) climb (n./v.)	
increase dramatically		soar (v.)
clearly (adv.)		it is evident from the information provided that
	interestingly (adv.)	it is interesting to note that
internet shopping	online shopping	
	Britain (n.) the UK	

Test Your Comprehension 综合练习

Answer these questions by circling A, B or C

1. Which of these synonyms should only be used when speaking?
   A. happen
   B. occur
   C. take place

2. Which sentence is correct?
   A. British had the most internet users.
   B. Britain have the most internet users.
   C. Britain had the most internet users.

3. "***Staggering***" (see Model Answer B) means:
   A. only
   B. very big
   C. stumbling

4. Which of these sentences is not correct?
   A. The number of people using the Internet increased threefold.
   B. There was a threefold increase in internet use.
   C. Internet use have threefold increased.

Answer these questions by writing YES or NO

5. "***Internet***" always starts with a CAPITAL LETTER.

6. You must always put "***the***" before "***Internet***".

7. "***A threefold increase***" (see Model Answer B) is a 300 percent increase.

8. "***Meanwhile***" (see both model answers) should always come at the start of a sentence.

9. Internet use in France doubled between 2000 and 2004.

Check your answers

1. **A**
   "***Take place***" and "***occur***" are good words to use in formal writing such as academic essays. "***Happen***" is better used when speaking or writing informally.

2. **C**
   "***Britain***" is a place; "***British***" is an adjective for people or things from Britain.

3. **B**
   "***Stagger***" sometimes means "***stumble***", but in this case "***staggering***" means "***very large***".

4. **C**

5. **NO**
   When you use "***Internet***" as a noun you must use a capital letter, but when you use it as an adjective you should not.

6. **NO**
   You should only use "***the***" if "***internet***" is a noun, not if it is an adjective. So the sentence, "***Many internet users shop on the Internet***" is correct.

7. **YES**
   "***A threefold increase***" is a 300 percent increase. Similarly, "***a twofold increase***" is a 200 percent increase, "***a fourfold increase***" is a 400 percent increase and so on.

8. **NO**
   "***Meanwhile***" goes at the start of the sentence in Model Answer A, but after the subject in Model Answer B. Model Answer B is better.

9. **YES**

Table
表格

Question 5 World Metro (MRT) Systems
全球地铁系统

WRITING TASK 1

You should spend about 20 minutes on this task.

The table below provides statistics on several major metro (MRT) systems around the world.

Summarise the information by selecting and reporting the main features, and make comparisons where relevant.

Write at least 150 words.

City	Year Completed	Total Length (km)	Carrying Capacity Per Year (millions)
London	1863	1100	548
Paris	1890	594	850
Tokyo	1904	149	1434
Washington DC	1921	114	70
Kyoto	1980	11	11
Los Angeles	2001	14	90

Model Answer A: IELTS Band 5^+

The table given compares the age, length and annual carrying capacity of metro systems in London, Paris, Tokyo, Washington DC, Kyoto and Los Angeles.

It is clear that the newer metro systems are generally much shorter than the older ones. The oldest metro system is that of London. It was built in 1863 and is 1100 kilometres long. Meanwhile, the second oldest metro system is in Paris. This metro was built in 1890 and is also the second longest, at 594 kilometres. On the other hand, the Kyoto and Los Angeles metro systems are much newer and shorter. They were built in 1980 and 2001, and are just 11 and 14 kilometres in length respectively.

We can also see from the table that the carrying capacities of these six metro systems are very different. The Tokyo metro system can carry the most people each year, at 1434 million. The Paris metro comes second, with 850 million. By contrast, the metro systems with the smallest carrying capacities are in Kyoto and Washington DC. These two metros can only carry 11 million and 70 million people per year respectively.

(187 words)

7+ 分

Model Answer B: IELTS Band 7^+

A glance at the table provided reveals a number of clear differences between the major metro systems of the world in terms of age, scale and annual carrying capacity.

One particularly interesting fact highlighted by the figure is that the more recently established metro systems are considerably shorter than the older ones. Completed in 1863, the London underground is the oldest of the metro systems listed and also the longest, extending for 1100 kilometres. Likewise, the second oldest system is also the second longest: built in 1890, the Paris metro is some 594 kilometres in length. In stark contrast, however, the Kyoto and Los Angeles metro systems—established in 1980 and 2001 respectively—are far shorter. The former covers a mere 11 kilometres and the latter just 14 kilometres.

With regard to yearly carrying capacity, the metro systems mentioned in the table vary greatly. The Tokyo metro is equipped to carry the largest number of passengers, at 1434 million. With 850 million, meanwhile, the Paris metro has the second largest carrying capacity. The systems with the smallest capacities are those of Kyoto and Washington DC, transporting just 11 million and 70 million people per year respectively.

(196 words)

Model Sentence Structures 句型示范

Sentence 1	IELTS 5	Interestingly, the newer metro systems are much shorter than the older ones.
	IELTS 6	It is interesting to note that the more recently established metro systems are far shorter than the older ones.
	IELTS 7+	One particularly interesting fact highlighted by the figure is that the more recently established metro systems are considerably shorter than the older ones.
Sentence 2	IELTS 5	The London metro was finished in 1863. It is the oldest metro system in the table and also the longest, at 1100 *kilometres.
	IELTS 6	The London underground was completed in 1863. It is the oldest of the metro systems listed and also the longest, stretching for 1100 kilometres.
	IELTS 7+	Completed in 1863, the London underground is the oldest of the metro systems listed and also the longest, extending for 1100 kilometres.
Sentence 3	IELTS 5	The metro systems mentioned in the table are very different in terms of how many passengers they can transport each year.
	IELTS 6	The metro systems mentioned vary greatly with regard to yearly carrying capacity.
	IELTS 7+	With regard to yearly carrying capacity, the metro systems mentioned in the table vary greatly.

Sentence 4	IELTS 5	At the same time, the Paris metro can transport the second largest number of people, at 850 million.
	IELTS 6	Meanwhile, the Paris metro has the second largest carrying capacity, with 850 million.
	IELTS 7+	With 850 million, meanwhile, the Paris metro has the second largest carrying capacity.

Note: This word is spelt "kilometre" in British/Australian English, but "kilometer" in American English. Other examples of this difference in spelling are "centre/center", "metre/meter" and "theatre/theater".

Academic Vocabulary 高分词汇

Basic 基础 5+分	Intermediate 中级 6+分	Advanced 高级 7+分
new (adj.)		recently established
	yearly (adj./adv.)	annual (adj.)
are very different		vary greatly
much (shorter)	far (shorter)	considerably (shorter)
on the other hand	by contrast	in stark contrast, however, ...
build (v.)		establish (v.)
length (n.)		scale (n.)
transport (n./v.)	carry (v.)	

Test Your Comprehension 综合练习

Answer these questions by circling A, B or C

Questions 1-3 relate to the following two statements from Model Answer B.

> A. **The more recently established metro systems are considerably shorter than the older ones.**
>
> B. **The London underground is the oldest of the metro systems listed and also the longest, extending for 1100 kilometres.**

1. Which is the most general statement?

2. Which statement is an example?

3. Which statement goes at the start of a paragraph?

4. In Model Answer B, "***completed***" means:
   A. finished
   B. 100 percent
   C. complex

Answer these questions by writing YES or NO

5. "***The table given compares***" (see Model Answer A) means "***the table which the examiner has given to me compares***".

6. The Paris metro is the third oldest metro (see both model answers).

7. "***The former***" refers to the Kyoto metro system while "***the latter***" means the Los Angeles metro (see Model Answer B).

8. "***With regard to***" (see Model Answer B) means "***about***" and is often used to start talking about a new subject.

9. "***The Kyoto metro system can carry 11 millions of passengers per year***" is grammatically correct.

Check your answers

1. **A**

This statement does not mention names or numbers.

2. **B**

The London metro is an example of an old and long metro system.

3. **A**

This kind of general sentence at the start of a paragraph is called a topic sentence. It is a very good idea for you to practise writing a topic sentence at the start of every paragraph you write, then giving examples and supporting information later.

4. **A**

5. **YES**

The word "***given***" makes the sentence structure a little more complex and interesting. Other ways to say the same thing are "***provided***" and "***supplied***".

6. **NO**

It is the second oldest.

7. **YES**

"***The former***" means "***the first one that I mentioned***", while "***the latter***" means "***the last one that I said***". Use these words if you talk about two different places or things. For example, "***Sydney is the largest city in Australia. Melbourne is second. The former is in the state of New South Wales, while the latter is in Victoria***".

8. **YES**

"***With regard to***" is a very good phrase to use in academic writing.

9. **NO**

You should write "***The Kyoto metro system can carry 11 million passengers per year***".

Column Graph
柱状图

Question 6 Global Education Rates
全球教育率

WRITING TASK 1

You should spend about 20 minutes on this task.

> ***The graphs below show current rates of secondary and higher education among people in various parts of the world.***
>
> ***Summarise the information by selecting and reporting the main features, and make comparisons where relevant.***

Write at least 150 words.

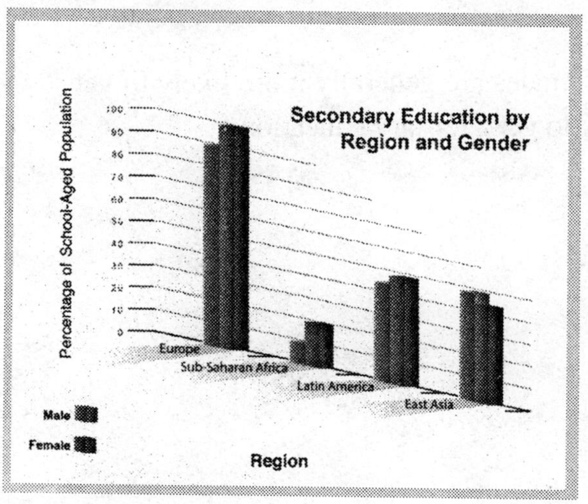

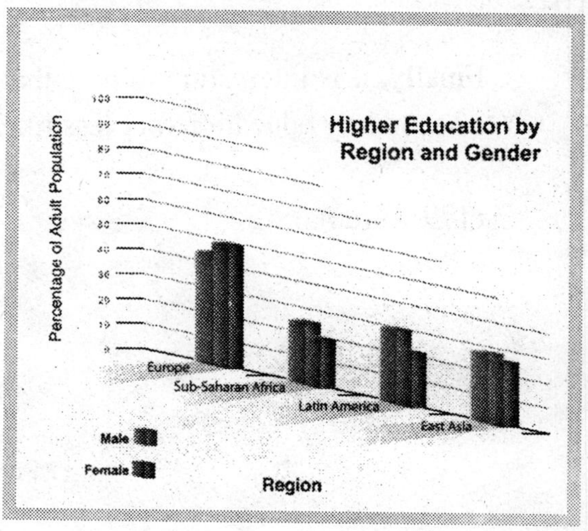

Model Answer A: IELTS Band 5+

The graphs provided show the percentages of males and females with secondary and higher education in four parts of the world.

Clearly, Europe has much higher levels of education in general than any other region. While 100 percent of school-aged girls and 90 percent of school-aged boys in Europe get a secondary education, the figures for girls and boys in Sub-Saharan Africa are just 20 and 10 percent. Meanwhile, the figures for Latin America and East Asia are between 40 and 50 percent.

We can also see from the graphs that higher education is more common in Europe. About 50 percent of adult females and 45 percent of adult males in this region have a higher education. By contrast, just 20 percent of women and 25 percent of men in Sub-Saharan Africa have this level of education. The figures for Latin America and East Asia are only a little higher than those for Africa.

Finally, it is interesting to note that females are generally more likely to get a secondary education, but less likely to get a tertiary education.

(179 words)

Model Answer B: IELTS Band 7⁺

Given are two column graphs comparing the rates of secondary and tertiary education among males and females in various different parts of the world.

While Europe enjoys relatively high levels of education overall, it seems that people in less affluent regions are far less likely to be educated. All European girls of school age and 90 percent of boys receive a secondary education, compared with only 20 percent of girls and 10 percent of boys in Sub-Saharan Africa. Latin America and East Asia, meanwhile, have moderate levels of secondary education—between 40 and 50 percent for both sexes.

With regard to higher education, the figures are much lower throughout the world. In Europe, some 50 percent of adult females and 45 percent of adult males gain a higher education. Conversely, only 20 percent of females and 25 percent of males in Sub-Saharan Africa attend college or university. The figures for Latin America and East Asia are marginally higher than those of Africa.

Also noteworthy is the fact that females are more likely to receive a secondary education in all regions except East Asia, but less likely to receive a tertiary education in all regions except Europe.

(196 words)

Model Sentence Structures 句型示范

Sentence 1	IELTS 5	Generally, Europe has quite high levels of education. However, it seems that far fewer people in poorer parts of the world get an education.
	IELTS 6	Overall, Europe enjoys relatively high levels of education. However, it seems that people in less affluent regions are much less likely to be educated.
	IELTS 7+	While Europe enjoys relatively high levels of education overall, it seems that people in less affluent regions are far less likely to be educated.
Sentence 2	IELTS 5	Levels of higher education are much lower in all parts of the world.
	IELTS 6	The figures for higher education are much lower throughout the world.
	IELTS 7+	With regard to higher education, the figures are much lower throughout the world.
Sentence 3	IELTS 6	On the other hand, just 20 percent of women and 25 percent of men in Sub-Saharan Africa go to college or university.
	IELTS 7+	Conversely, only 20 percent of females and 25 percent of males in Sub-Saharan Africa attend college or university.

Sentence 4	**IELTS 5**	It is also important to note that more girls go to high school in all parts of the world except East Asia.
	IELTS 6	It is also worth noting that females are more likely to attend secondary school in all regions except East Asia.
	IELTS 7+	Also noteworthy is the fact that females are more likely to receive a secondary education in all regions except East Asia.

Academic Vocabulary 高分词汇

Basic 基础	Intermediate 中级	Advanced 高级
	higher education	tertiary education
get (v.)		receive (v.)
		gain an education/ receive an education
		gain a higher education/ attend college or university
	in general overall (adv.)	
woman (n.)	female (n./adj.)	
man (n.)	male (n./adj.)	
a little		marginally (adv.)
	part of the world	region of the world
		conversely (adv.) by contrast
	percentage (n.) rate (n.)	

Test Your Comprehension 综合练习

Answer these questions by circling A, B or C

Questions 1-3 relate to the following two statements from Model Answer B.

> A. **All European girls of school age and 90 percent of boys receive a secondary education.**
> B. **Europe enjoys relatively high levels of education overall.**

1. Which is the most general statement (the topic sentence)?

2. Which statement is an example?

3. Which statement should be placed at the start of a paragraph?

4. In these two essays, "***figure***" means:
   A. number
   B. graph
   C. both graph and number

5. Which of these is incorrect?
   A. We can also see from the graphs...
   B. We can also find from the graphs...
   C. According to the graphs...

6. In Model Answer B, "***relatively***" means:
   A. quite
   B. like family
   C. very

7. In Model Answer B, "***affluent***" means:
   A. poor
   B. rich
   C. not fluent

8. Which of the following phrases is wrong?
   A. between 40 and 50 percent
   B. from 40 to 50 percent
   C. between 40 to 50 percent

Answer these questions by writing YES or NO

9. "***Throughout the world***" (see Model Answer B) means "***worldwide***".

10. "***School***" and "***university***" are the same thing.

11. The most impoverished region has the lowest rate of university attendance.

Check your answers

1. **B**

   There are no percentages or other specific details in this sentence.

2. **A**

   "***All European girls of school age and 90 percent of boys***" is a good example of Europe's high level of education.

3. **B**

   This is the topic sentence of paragraph 2.

4. **C**

   "***Figure***" has two meanings.

5. **B**

   "***We can find***" is wrong.

6. **A**

   Other words for "***relatively***" include "***comparatively***" and "***rather***". The word "***relative***" means "***family member***".

7. **B**

   Another word for "***affluent***" is "***wealthy***". A good way to write "***poor***" is "***impoverished***".

8. **C**

   The word "***between***" should not go with "***to***".

9. **YES**

   Make sure you spell "***worldwide***" correctly. "***Worldwild***" is wrong.

10. **NO**

    In American English the words "***school***" and "***university***" can mean the same thing. However, in British/Australian English "***school***" means "***primary school***" or "***high school***". A "***university***" is a place where you go to get a higher education after you graduate from "***school***".

11. **YES**

    Sub-Saharan Africa is the poorest region of the world and it has the lowest rate of university attendance.

Bar Graph

条状图

Question 7 Plastic Surgery in Korea 韩国的整形手术

WRITING TASK 1

You should spend about 20 minutes on this task.

The graphs below compare the number of cosmetic procedures performed on males and females in Korea in 2004.

Summarise the information by selecting and reporting the main features, and make comparisons where relevant.

Write at least 150 words.

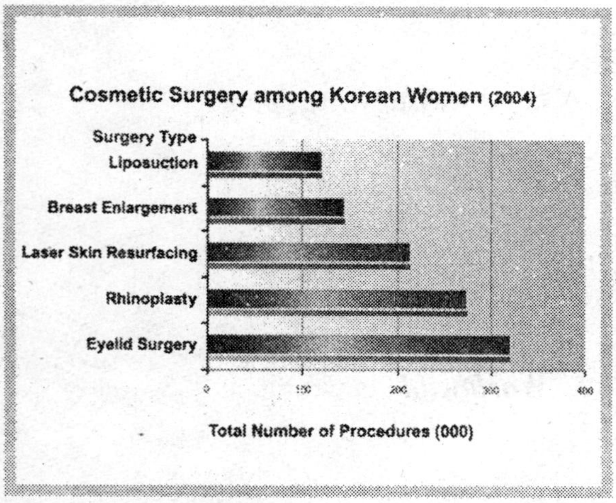

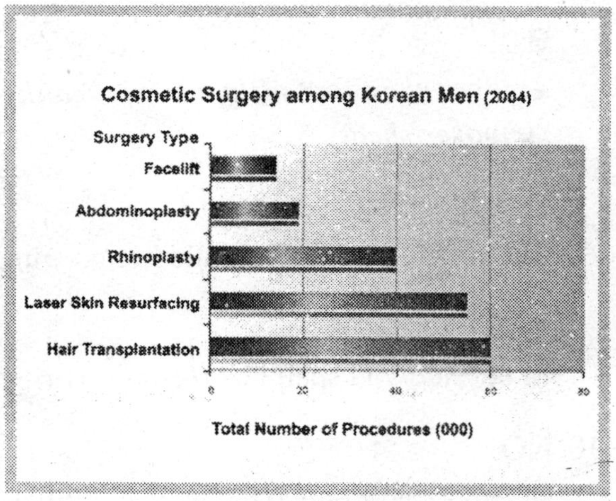

5⁺分

Model Answer A: IELTS Band 5⁺

The two graphs provided show how popular different kinds of plastic surgery were among Korean men and women in 2004.

It is clear that plastic surgery was quite popular among women. The most common types of surgery for this group were eyelid surgery and rhinoplasty, with 320,000 and 275,000 operations respectively. Laser skin resurfacing was third, at 215,000. Meanwhile, breast enlargement and liposuction were a little less common. There were just 145,000 and 120,000 of these operations.

As for Korean men, most kinds of plastic surgery were much less popular. Hair transplantation was the most common type of surgery for this group; however, there were only 60,000 of these operations. The second most popular kind of plastic surgery for men was laser skin resurfacing, with 55,000 operations. Rhinoplasty was the third most common, at 40,000 operations. Last of all, abdominoplasty and facelifts were much less popular—there were just 19,000 and 14,000 of these operations respectively.

Interestingly, no hair transplantation, abdominoplasty or facelift operations were reported among Korean women in 2004. Similarly, no liposuction, breast enlargement or eyelid surgery procedures were conducted on men.

(184 words)

Model Answer B: IELTS Band 7^{+}

A glance at the two figures provided reveals the popularity of various forms of cosmetic surgery among Korean men and women in 2004.

Not surprisingly, plastic surgery enjoyed widespread popularity among women. By far the most common forms of cosmetic procedure for this group, eyelid surgery and rhinoplasty were performed a staggering 320,000 and 275,000 times respectively. Third in terms of popularity, meanwhile, was laser skin resurfacing. An approximate 215,000 of these procedures were conducted on women during the year in question. Breast enlargement and liposuction were considerably less common, at 145,000 and 120,000 operations respectively.

Equally predictable is the fact that plastic surgery was far less popular among men. In contrast to women, hair transplantation was the most common cosmetic procedure. There were just 60,000 of these operations among Korean males. Numbering some 55,000 procedures, laser skin resurfacing was second for this group. Third was rhinoplasty, at approximately 40,000 operations. Finally, a relatively small 19,000 abdominoplasty and 14,000 facelift procedures were carried out on men during 2004.

It is interesting to note that hair transplantation, abdominoplasty and facelift patients were exclusively male, while 100 percent of liposuction, breast enlargement and eyelid surgery patients were female.

(196 words)

Model Sentence Structures 句型示范

Sentence 1	**IELTS 6**	It is not surprising to see that plastic surgery was quite popular among women.
	IELTS 7+	Not surprisingly, plastic surgery enjoyed widespread popularity among women.
Sentence 2	**IELTS 5**	Eyelid surgery and rhinoplasty were the most common types of plastic surgery for this group. There were 320,000 and 275,000 of these operations.
	IELTS 6	Eyelid surgery and rhinoplasty were by far the most common forms of cosmetic procedure for this group. These operations were performed a staggering 320,000 and 275,000 times.
	IELTS 7+	By far the most common forms of cosmetic procedure for this group, eyelid surgery and rhinoplasty were performed a staggering 320,000 and 275,000 times respectively.
Sentence 3	**IELTS 5**	Laser skin resurfacing was the second most popular type of plastic surgery for this group, at about 55,000 procedures.
	IELTS 6	Laser skin resurfacing was second for this group, numbering some 55,000 procedures.
	IELTS 7+	Numbering some 55,000 procedures, laser skin resurfacing was second for this group.

Academic Vocabulary 高分词汇

Basic 基础 5+分	Intermediate 中级 6+分	Advanced 高级 7+分
graph (n./v.)		figure (n.)
kind (n.) type (n.)		form (n.)
different kinds		various forms
	some (adv.)	approximately (adv.) an approximate
		conduct (v.) perform (v.) carry out
	not surprising	predictable (adj.)
	common (adj.) popular (adj.)	
much less popular	far less popular	considerably less common
	operation (n.)	procedure (n.)
	plastic surgery	cosmetic procedure/ cosmetic surgery
	interestingly (adv.)	it is interesting to note that
woman (n.)	female (n./adj.)	
man (n.)	male (n./adj.)	

Test Your Comprehension 综合练习

Answer these questions by circling A, B or C

Questions 1-3 relate to the following two statements from Model Answer B.

> A. **Eyelid surgery and rhinoplasty were performed a staggering 320,000 and 275,000 times respectively.**
> B. **Plastic surgery enjoyed widespread popularity among women.**

1. Which statement is the topic sentence (the sentence that introduces a new idea in a general way)?

2. Which statement comes at the start of a paragraph?

3. Which statement gives examples of different kinds of plastic surgery?

4. Which of these words does not belong in this list? Why not?
   A. eyelid surgery
   B. abdominoplasty
   C. plastic surgery

5. How many verb tenses does the writer use in these essays?
   A. one
   B. two
   C. three

Answer these questions by writing YES or NO

6. The two model answers discuss men and women in the same paragraph.

7. In Model Answer A, the writer says "***as for Korean men***" after he has finished discussing Korean women.

8. In Model Answer B, "***Hair transplantation ... patients were exclusively male***" means that most hair transplant patients were men.

9. These essays have no conclusion.

Check your answers

1. **B**

   This statement introduces the topic of plastic surgery and women.

2. **B**

   This sentence comes at the start of paragraph 2.

3. **A**

   The two examples given are "***eyelid surgery***" and "***rhinoplasty***".

4. **C**

   "***Plastic surgery***" is a category, whereas "***eyelid surgery***" and "***abdominoplasty***" are examples of it. Category words or phrases are best used at the start of a paragraph, in the topic sentence.

5. **B**

   The writer uses present tense to talk about the graphs and past tense to discuss trends in plastic surgery in 2004. Note the verb tenses used in the phrases, "***a glance at the two figures provided reveals***" and "***it is clear that***".

6. **NO**

   Each new topic needs a new paragraph—one paragraph is written about men and one is written about women.

7. **YES**

   "***As for Korean men***" is the same as "***with regard to Korean men***". This is a good way to change the subject.

8. **NO**

   It actually means that all hair transplant patients were men.

9. **YES**

   It is not necessary to write a conclusion for Writing Task 1. Instead, you may choose to highlight a point that you think is interesting.

Diagram

流程图

Question 8 River Pollution 河流污染

WRITING TASK 1

You should spend about 20 minutes on this task.

> ***The diagram below shows what happens to pollutants from farming and industry once in a river system.***
>
> ***Summarise the information by selecting and reporting the main features, and make comparisons where relevant.***

Write at least 150 words.

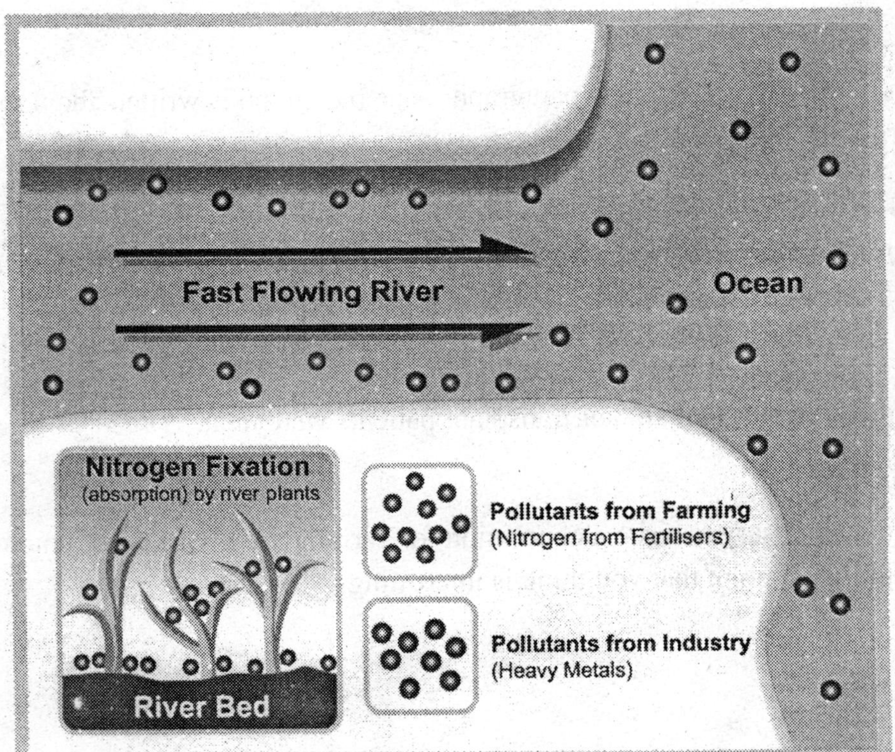

Model Answer A: IELTS Band 5^+

The diagram given shows a river flowing quickly towards the ocean and what happens to two different kinds of pollutants when they enter it. The pollutants that are mentioned in the diagram are fertilisers from farming and heavy metals from industry. The fertilisers are shown as blue spots, while the heavy metals are shown as black spots.

It is clear that the pollutants from industry stay in the river for a longer period of time than the pollutants from farming. According to the diagram, plants growing on the river bed remove fertilisers from the water through a process called nitrogen fixation. However, they do not absorb heavy metals in the same way. These industrial pollutants either sit on the bottom of the river or flow into the sea.

Therefore, the effects of heavy metals on the environment probably continue for longer than those of fertilisers.

(145 words)

Model Answer B: IELTS Band 7^{+}

Given is a diagram illustrating the interaction between two types of pollutants—namely fertilisers from farming and heavy metals produced by industry—and the ecosystem of a fast flowing river. The fertilisers are denoted by blue spots, while the heavy metals are marked as black spots.

From the information supplied, it is evident that fertilisers are more readily removed from the water through natural processes than heavy metals, and that the latter tend to remain in a river system for much longer periods of time. In the lower section of the diagram, plants growing on the river bed are shown to absorb fertilisers from the water through a process known as nitrogen fixation. By contrast, heavy metals are not filtered from the river system in this way and instead either settle on the bottom or are emptied into the sea.

Thus, it is reasonable to surmise that the effect of heavy metals on the environment is longer lasting than that of fertilisers.

(162 words)

Model Sentence Structures 句型示范

Sentence 1	IELTS 5	The blue spots show fertilisers. At the same time, the black spots denote heavy metals.
	IELTS 6	The fertilisers are shown as blue spots. Meanwhile, the heavy metals are denoted by black spots.
	IELTS 7+	The fertilisers are denoted by blue spots, while the heavy metals are marked as black spots.
Sentence 2	IELTS 5	The diagram clearly shows that natural processes in the river take fertilisers out of the water much more quickly and easily than heavy metals. These heavy metals usually stay in the river system for much longer.
	IELTS 6	From the information supplied, it is clear that natural processes in the river remove fertilisers from the water much more readily than heavy metals, and that these heavy metals tend to remain in the water for much longer periods of time.
	IELTS 7+	From the information supplied, it is evident that fertilisers are more readily removed from the water through natural processes than heavy metals, and that the latter tend to remain in a river system for much longer periods of time.

Sentence 3	IELTS 5	The lower part of the diagram shows that river plants take fertilisers out of the water through nitrogen fixation.
	IELTS 6	The lower section of the diagram shows that plants growing on the river bed absorb fertilisers from the water through a process called nitrogen fixation.
	IELTS 7+	In the lower section of the diagram, plants growing on the river bed are shown to absorb fertilisers from the water through a process known as nitrogen fixation.
Sentence 4	IELTS 5	On the other hand, plants do not remove heavy metals from the river system in the same way.
	IELTS 6	By contrast, plants do not filter heavy metals from the river system in this way.
	IELTS 7+	By contrast, heavy metals are not filtered from the river system in this way.

Academic Vocabulary 高分词汇

Basic 基础 5⁺分	Intermediate 中级 6⁺分	Advanced 高级 7⁺分
*show (v.)		illustrate (v.)
*show (v.)	mark (v.)	denote (v.)
give (v.)	supply (n./v.)	
stay (v.)	remain (v.)	
	according to the diagram/ the diagram given shows	
clear (adj.)		evident (adj.)
sit (v.)		settle (v.)
	remove (v.)	absorb (v.) filter (n./v.)
	therefore (adv.)	thus (adv.)

Note: 1. "Show" means "reveal". E.g. "This catalogue shows how much a TV costs."
2. "Show" means "stand for" or "symbolise". E.g. "The symbol $ (the dollar sign) shows money."

Test Your Comprehension 综合练习

Answer these questions by circling A, B or C

1. What is the main idea of these two essays?
   A. Heavy metals are worse for the environment than fertilisers.
   B. Fertilisers and heavy metals are equally bad for the environment.
   C. Rivers carry fertilisers and heavy metals towards the sea.

2. Which is the American spelling?
   A. fertiliser
   B. fertilizer

3. In Model Answer B, the word "***readily***" means:
   A. quickly and easily
   B. gradually
   C. sometimes

Answer these questions by writing YES or NO

4. The writer only uses past tense in these essays.

5. "***Surmise***" (see Model Answer B) is a more formal word for "***guess***".

6. In Model Answer B, "***tend to***" means "***seldom***".

7. Model Answer A is not long enough to get a good score in the real test.

Check your answers

1. **A**

2. **B**

   You can use either American spelling or British/Australian spelling, but you should try to be consistent. Choose one, not both.

3. **A**

4. **NO**

   In fact, the writer only uses present tense in these model answers because there is no year given to indicate that this information is taken from the past. You should use present tense in most diagram questions.

5. **YES**

   "***Surmise***" is a good word to use in academic English.

6. **NO**

   "***Tend to***" means "***frequently***" or "***often***". It is used to talk about a typical occurrence or trend.

7. **NO**

   It all depends on the question. In this case, it only took 145 words to describe the diagram completely. The length of your essay is just one thing the examiner looks at, so if your essay is a little short you can still get a good score.

Diagram (Flow Chart)
流程图

Question 9 Mobile Phone Recycling
手机回收

WRITING TASK 1

You should spend about 20 minutes on this task.

The following is a diagram of the mobile phone recycling process.

Summarise the information by selecting and reporting the main features, and make comparisons where relevant.

Write at least 150 words.

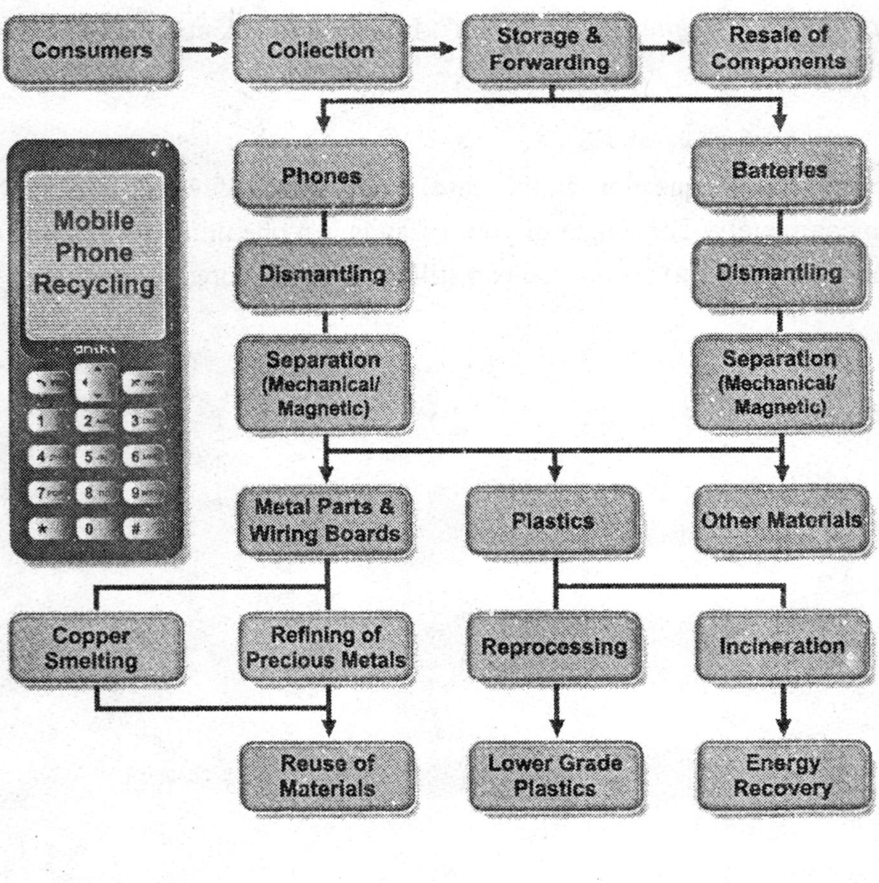

Model Answer A: IELTS Band 5⁺

The diagram given shows how mobile phones are recycled. Clearly, the recycling process has three main stages.

In the first stage of the process, the recycling company collects mobile phones from consumers. Then it stores or forwards the phones and resells some of the components.

In the second stage of the recycling process, the company separates the mobile phones from their batteries and dismantles both of these. Then it separates the phones and the batteries into mechanical and magnetic parts. After this, it divides these parts up into different kinds of material. The kinds of material that are mentioned in the diagram are metals parts and wiring boards, plastics and other materials.

In the third part of the process, the recycling company removes copper and precious metals from the metal parts. It smelts the copper and refines the precious metals. Then it reuses these materials. As for the plastic parts, it reprocesses some of these into lower grade plastics and incinerates the rest of them to recover energy. The diagram does not show what happens to the other materials.

(179 words)

Model Answer B: IELTS Band 7^{+}

Given is a diagram illustrating the process by which mobile phones are recycled. It is evident from the information provided that there are three main phases involved.

Prior to the actual processing of the phones, it is first necessary for the recycler to collect them from consumers. They are then either placed into storage or forwarded directly. At this point, the resale of certain components occurs.

The second stage of the recycling process, meanwhile, entails the separation of the mobile phones from their batteries and the dismantling of both. Having further separated the phones and batteries into mechanical and magnetic parts, these parts are then divided into metals, plastics and other materials.

In the third and final phase, copper and precious metals are extracted from the metal components. The former is smelted while the latter are refined and the raw materials produced through these processes are subsequently reused. Meanwhile, plastic parts are either converted into lower grade plastics or incinerated to recover energy. The diagram does not indicate how other kinds of material are disposed of.

(176 words)

Model Sentence Structures 句型示范

Sentence 1	IELTS 5	The diagram given shows how mobile phones are recycled.
	IELTS 6	The diagram given illustrates the process by which mobile phones are recycled.
	IELTS 7+	Given is a diagram illustrating the process by which mobile phones are recycled.
Sentence 2	IELTS 5	The recycling company has to collect the phones from consumers before it actually processes them.
	IELTS 6	Before it actually processes the phones, the recycler first has to collect them from consumers.
	IELTS 7+	Prior to the actual processing of the phones, it is first necessary for the recycler to collect them from consumers.
Sentence 3	IELTS 5	Then the recycling company resells some of the parts.
	IELTS 6	Some of the components are then resold (by the recycling company).
	IELTS 7+	At this point, the resale of certain components occurs.
Sentence 4	IELTS 5	The recycler separates the phones and batteries into mechanical and magnetic parts. Then it divides these parts into metals, plastics and other materials.
	IELTS 6	After separating the phones and batteries into mechanical and magnetic parts, the recycler then divides them into metals, plastics and other materials.
	IELTS 7+	Having separated the phones and batteries into mechanical and magnetic parts, these parts are then divided into metals, plastics and other materials.

Academic Vocabulary 高分词汇

Basic 基础 5+分	Intermediate 中级 6分	Advanced 高级 7+分
	recycling company recycler (n.)	
	involve (v.)	entail (v.)
part (n.)	stage (n.)	phase (n.)
then (adv.)	after this	subsequently (adv.) at this point
	divide (v.) separate (v.)	
part (n.)		component (n.)
	remove (v.)	extract (v.)
show (v.)		indicate (v.)

Test Your Comprehension 综合练习

Answer these questions by circling A, B or C

1. Which of the following sentences is grammatically correct?
   A. The recycling company collect mobile phones from customers.
   B. The recycle company collects mobile phones from customers.
   C. The recycling company collects mobile phones from customers.

2. In Model Answer B, "***convert***" means:
   A. transform
   B. mix
   C. recycle

3. "***Dispose of***" (see Model Answer B) is a more formal way to say:
   A. sell
   B. throw away
   C. keep

4. In Model Answer B, "***the former***" refers to:
   A. precious metals
   B. copper
   C. mobile phones

5. "***Prior to***" (see Model Answer B) is a more formal way to say:
   A. before
   B. after
   C. during

Answer these questions by writing YES or NO

6. In Model Answer A, the writer begins too many sentences with "***the recycling company***", "***the company***" or "***it***".

7. "***Dismantle***" is a less formal word for "***build***" (see both model answers).

8. "***Place***" (see Model Answer B) is a word we often use for "***put***" in spoken English.

9. The dismantling phase precedes the separation phase.

Check your answers

1. **C**

"***My brother***" is "***he***"; "***your friends***" are "***they***"; and "***the recycling company***" is "***it***". Therefore, the verb "***collect***" must take an "***s***".

2. **A**

The writer uses the word "***convert***" followed by "***into***". In most cases, you must use both. So you could write, "***Freezers convert water into ice***".

3. **B**

The phrase "***dispose of***" means "***get rid of***" or "***throw away***". It is very useful in academic writing, especially when describing diagrams or flow charts. Do not forget "***of***". For instance, "***Old furniture can be difficult to dispose of***".

4. **B**

In the model answer, "***the former***" refers to "***copper***"; "***the latter***" means "***precious metals***".

5. **A**

6. **YES**

Model Answer A contains too many active sentences. When describing diagrams, it is a good idea to try writing more passive sentences.

7. **NO**

The word "***dismantle***" is a more formal word for "***take apart***".

8. **NO**

Use "***put***" when speaking and "***place***" when writing.

9. **YES**

The dismantling phase comes before the separation phase.

Diagram (Map)

地图

Question 10 Planned Shopping Centre Locations

购物中心预定地

WRITING TASK 1

You should spend about 20 minutes on this task.

The figure below is a town planning map, showing the likely positions of two new shopping centres as well as the various different zones and major transportation routes of the town.

Summarise the information by selecting and reporting the main features, and make comparisons where relevant.

Write at least 150 words.

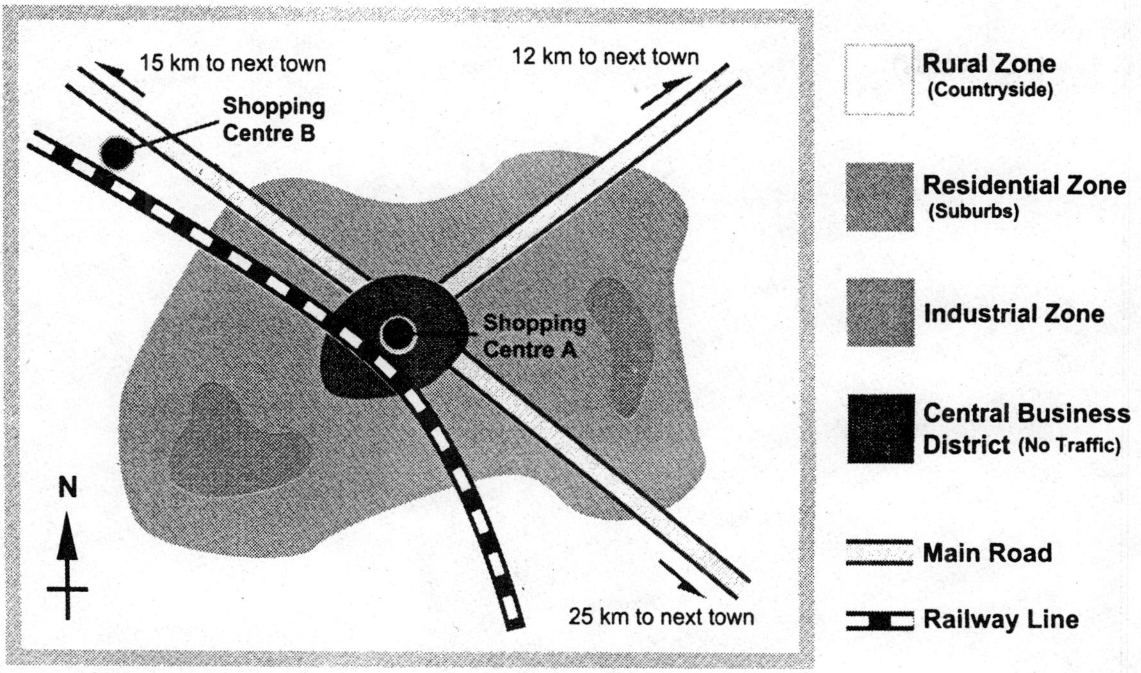

Model Answer A: IELTS Band 5+

This is a map of a town showing where two new shopping centres will probably be built as well as different zones and transportation routes.

In the middle of the town there is a small zone called the central business district. Cars are not allowed in this zone. Outside the central business district there is a large residential zone and outside this there is an even larger rural zone. There is also a railway line running right through the town and three main roads which start on the edge of the central business district and go to nearby towns.

According to the diagram, one shopping centre will probably be built in the middle of the town while the other one will be built in the northwest rural area. People will be able to get to the first shopping centre by train or park their cars on the edge of the central business district and walk to it. Meanwhile they will be able to get to the second shopping centre by car or train because it will be located between the railway line and the main northwest road.

(187 words)

Model Answer B: IELTS Band 7+

Given is a map of an unnamed town illustrating the probable sites of two new shopping centres in relation to various different zones as well as major transportation links.

As shown in the figure, the town has four main zones. Located at the apex of three arterial roads is a relatively small central business district. Cars are not permitted in this area and all major roads terminate at its outer edge. Surrounding the town centre is a much larger residential zone which has within it two smaller industrial zones. Beyond this, meanwhile, is an even larger rural area. A railway line runs through the entire town from the northwest to the southeast.

With regard to the planned locations of the two new shopping centres, one is likely to be situated in the town centre and will be accessible by train or by parking on the edge of the central business district and walking. The other will probably be placed on the outskirts of the town to the northwest. Access to this shopping centre will be by either car or train as it will be situated between the railway line and the main northwest road.

(194 words)

Model Sentence Structures 句型示范

Sentence 1	IELTS 5	There is a small central business district at the intersection of three main roads.
	IELTS 6	There is a relatively small central business district located at the apex of three arterial roads.
	IELTS 7+	Located at the apex of three arterial roads is a relatively small central business district.
Sentence 2	IELTS 5	At the same time, there is an even bigger rural area outside this.
	IELTS 6	Meanwhile, there is an even larger rural area beyond this.
	IELTS 7+	Beyond this, meanwhile, is an even larger rural area.
Sentence 3	IELTS 5	One of the new shopping centres will probably be located in the town centre and people will be able to visit it by train or by parking on the edge of the central business district and walking.
	IELTS 6	As for the locations of the two new shopping centres, one will probably be situated in the town centre and people will be able to access it by train or by parking on the edge of the central business district and walking.
	IELTS 7+	With regard to the planned locations of the two new shopping centres, one is likely to be situated in the town centre and will be accessible by train or by parking on the edge of the central business district and walking.

Sentence 4	IELTS 5	People will be able to get to this shopping centre by car or by train because it will be located between the railway line and the main northwest road.
	IELTS 6	People will be able to access this shopping centre by car or train as it will be situated between the railway line and the main northwest road.
	IELTS 7+	Access to this shopping centre will be by either car or train as it will be situated between the railway line and the main northwest road.

Academic Vocabulary 高分词汇

Basic 基础 5+分	Intermediate 中级 6+分	Advanced 高级 7+分
show (v.)		illustrate (v.)
	will probably	(be) likely to
	allow (v.)	permit (v.)
	(be) located	(be) placed (be) situated
middle (n.)	*centre (n.)	

Note: This word is spelt "centre" in British/Australian English, but "center" in American English. The pronunciation is virtually the same. Some other words that follow the same rule are "metre/meter", "litre/liter" and "theatre/theater".

Test Your Comprehension 综合练习

Answer these questions by circling A, B or C

Questions 1-3 relate to the following two statements from Model Answer B.

> A. **The town has four main zones.**
> B. **Located at the apex of three arterial roads is a relatively small central business district.**

1. Which sentence is more general?

2. Which statement should be placed at the beginning of a paragraph?

3. Which statement names one of the zones in the town?

4. What verb tense(s) does the writer use in these essays?
   A. future tense
   B. present tense
   C. present and future tense

5. The future tense form of "*can*" is:
   A. will be able to
   B. will can
   C. can going to

6. How many times does the writer start sentences with "*there is*" or "*there are*" in Model Answer A?
   A. 1
   B. 2
   C. 4

7. "*Rural area*" (see Model Answer B) is a more formal way to say:
   A. the city
   B. the country
   C. the suburbs

Answer these questions by writing YES or NO

8. In Model Answer B, "***terminate***" is a more formal way to say "***end***".

9. The word "***accessible***" (see Model Answer B) means that people can reach or get to a place or facility easily.

10. "***The outskirts of the town***" (see Model Answer B) refers to the "***city centre***".

Check your answers

1. **A**
   "***Four main zones***" is a general term.

2. **A**
   This statement is found at the start of Model Answer B paragraph 2. It is a topic sentence (a general sentence that introduces a paragraph).

3. **B**
   "***Central business district***" is one example of the "***four main zones***" mentioned in the topic sentence.

4. **C**
   The writer uses present tense to talk about the map and the town, but future tense to talk about the planned shopping centres and how people will access them.

5. **A**

6. **C**
   Model Answer A uses "***there is***" and "***there are***" too repetitively. Model Answer B is better because it has more variety.

7. **B**
   "***Rural***" is an adjective that means "***country***". A good adjective for "***city***" is "***urban***".

8. **YES**
   "***Terminate***" is a good word to use in academic writing.

9. **YES**
   The word "***access***" means "***reach***" or "***get to***".

10. **NO**
    "***The outskirts of town***" are the outer edges of a city.

IELTS

WRITE RIGHT

学术类和培训类写作 TASK 2

Writing Task 2:
Academic & General Training Modules

Question Types

In Writing Task 2 of both the Academic and General Training modules you will be expected to write 250 words or more expressing your opinion about a given topic. The vast majority of IELTS Writing Task 2 questions are about trends or problems in society. It is essential that you learn to distinguish between these two: global tourism is a trend because it has both positive and negative aspects (it is both good and bad), while pollution is a problem because it only has negative aspects (it is all bad). IELTS writing questions related to such societal trends and problems generally come in the following forms:

1. Do You Agree or Disagree?

需就题目提供的观点表达意见的题型

You may be asked whether you agree or disagree with a given statement and requested to give reasons for your answer. This type of question can be expressed in the following two ways:

Form A What are your opinions on this?

WRITING TASK 2

You should spend about 40 minutes on this task.

Write about the following topic:

> ***International tourism is now more common than ever before. Some feel that this is a positive trend, while others do not.***
>
> ***What are your opinions on this?***

Give reasons for your answer and include any relevant examples from your own knowledge or experience.

Write at least 250 words.

Form B Do you agree or disagree?

WRITING TASK 2

You should spend about 40 minutes on this task.

Write about the following topic:

> ***Men and women are different in terms of their characteristics and abilities. For this reason, some jobs are better done by men and others by women.***
>
> ***Do you agree or disagree?***

Give reasons for your answer and include any relevant examples from your own knowledge or experience.

Write at least 250 words.

2. Discuss Causes, Effects and/or Solutions.

需具体提出原因或解决方法的题型

Some IELTS writing tasks will require you to discuss the causes, effects and/or solutions to a topical, societal issue.

WRITING TASK 2

You should spend about 40 minutes on this task.

Write about the following topic:

> ***Many people believe that educational standards have declined in recent times, particularly in the areas of literacy and numeracy.***
>
> ***Discuss the causes of this problem and offer some possible solutions to it.***

Write at least 250 words.

What Are Your Opinions on This?

你的意见是什么?

Question 11 The Internet 网络

WRITING TASK 2

You should spend about 40 minutes on this task.

Write about the following topic:

> ***The Internet has dramatically altered our lives over the past few decades. Although some of these changes have been negative, the overall effect of this technology has been positive.***
>
> ***What are your opinions on this?***

Give reasons for your answer and include any relevant examples from your own knowledge or experience.

Write at least 250 words.

Model Answer A: IELTS Band 5^+

There are various different opinions on the subject of the Internet. While some people might suggest that it has negatively affected our lives and society, I personally believe that it has actually made the world a much better place. In my opinion, there are two main benefits to this technology.

Firstly, I am sure most people would agree that the Internet has improved the way we communicate. Although spending too much time using the Internet instead of talking to real people can cause social isolation, most of us have benefited greatly from e-mail and internet chat *programs like MSN Messenger. These useful and powerful communication tools have made it much faster, easier and cheaper to keep in touch with family and friends in other countries (and also to do international business).

In addition to this, the Internet provides us with all of the information in the world at work, school and home. In the past, research involved spending many hours in the library. Now, however, the same information is available online. Of course, not all of the material available on the Internet is true or useful. Much of the material on the Internet is offensive and some of it is dangerous—there is everything from pornography to instructions on how to make bombs. Nevertheless, I feel that this free movement and sharing of information has generally been beneficial.

To conclude, I once again restate my view that the Internet has had a positive influence on modern life because of its effects on both communication and the flow of information.

(259 words)

Note: Americans write "program", whereas the British/Australian spelling of this word is "programme". We all write "program" when we talk about "computer programs".

Model Answer B: IELTS Band 7^+

The Internet has brought significant changes to our lives in recent years. Yet, there remains some disagreement as to whether the overall effect of this technology has been positive or negative. While there are certainly valid arguments to the contrary, I personally believe that the benefits of the Internet far outweigh its drawbacks. These benefits are twofold.

First of all, it is an indisputable fact that the Internet has revolutionised the way we communicate. Despite the risk of social isolation—a problem occasionally seen in people who spend too much time at their computer terminal rather than relating to people in the real world—most of us have benefited greatly from e-mail and internet chat programs like MSN Messenger. These incredibly useful and powerful tools of communication facilitate both contact with loved ones in faraway places and global trade.

Equally importantly, though, the Internet has placed the entire world (and all of the information in it) at our fingertips. In earlier times, conducting research entailed long hours searching library shelves. Now, however, the same information can be accessed at the click of a button. Admittedly, not all of the information available on the Internet is reliable or helpful—there is a vast amount of material online that some would consider offensive or dangerous, ranging from pornography to instructions on how to make bombs. Nonetheless, I would contend that this free flow of information has generally been a very positive development.

By way of conclusion, I once again reaffirm my position that the Internet has had a positive impact on modern life because of its influence on communication and the flow of information.

(272 words)

Model Sentence Structures 句型示范

Sentence 1	IELTS 5	The Internet has dramatically changed our lives in recent times.
	IELTS 6	The Internet has caused dramatic changes in our lives in recent years.
	IELTS 7+	The Internet has brought significant changes to our lives in recent years.
Sentence 2	IELTS 5	But people still disagree about whether the effect of the Internet has been good or bad.
	IELTS 6	However, there is still some disagreement about whether the overall effect of the Internet has been good or bad.
	IELTS 7+	Yet, there remains some disagreement as to whether the overall effect of this technology has been positive or negative.
Sentence 3	IELTS 5	First, most people would agree that the Internet has improved the way we communicate.
	IELTS 6	Firstly, few people would disagree that the Internet has greatly improved the way we communicate.
	IELTS 7+	First of all, it is an indisputable fact that the Internet has revolutionised the way we communicate.

Sentence 4	IELTS 5	It is true that spending too much time using the Internet is dangerous because it can cause social problems. However, e-mail and internet chat programs like MSN Messenger have helped most of us.
	IELTS 6	Although there is some danger of social isolation (a problem that we sometimes see in people who spend too much time online instead of talking to real people), e-mail and internet chat programs like MSN Messenger have brought great benefits to most of us.
	IELTS 7+	Despite the risk of social isolation—a problem occasionally seen in people who spend too much time at their computer terminal rather than relating to people in the real world—most of us have benefited greatly from e-mail and internet chat programs like MSN Messenger.
Sentence 5	IELTS 5	But I feel that this free movement of information has been a very positive trend.
	IELTS 6	However, I would argue that this free movement of information has generally been a very positive trend.
	IELTS 7+	Nonetheless, I would contend that this free flow of information has generally been a very positive development.
Sentence 6	IELTS 6	In conclusion, I restate my opinion that the Internet has positively influenced modern life because of its effect on communications and the movement of information.
	IELTS 7+	By way of conclusion, I once again reaffirm my position that the Internet has had a positive impact on modern life because of its influence on communication and the flow of information.

Academic Vocabulary 高分词汇

Basic 基础 5+分	Intermediate 中级 6分	Advanced 高级 7分
opinion (n.)	position (n.)	
change (n./v.)		alter (v.)
affect (v.) effect (n.)	influence (v./n.)	impact (v./n.)
	believe (v.) feel (v.)	
	improve (v.)	*revolutionise (v.)
talk to		relate to
	communication (n.) contact (n./v.)	
	instead of	rather than
family and friends		loved ones
other countries		faraway places
	international business	global trade
	in the past	in earlier times
	involve (v.)	entail (v.)
	(be) available	can be accessed
	of course	admittedly (adv.)
	much of	a vast amount of
true (adj.)		reliable (adj.)
helpful (adj.) useful (adj.)		
		nevertheless (adv.) nonetheless (adv.)
	to conclude	by way of conclusion
		reaffirm (v.) restate (v.)

Note: This word is spelt "revolutionise" in British/Australian English but "revolutionize" in American English. Both are acceptable, but you should decide which form of English you want to use and be consistent. Other examples of this spelling difference are "organise/organize" and "realise/realize".

Test Your Comprehension 综合练习

Answer these questions by circling A, B or C

1. What is Question 11 about?

   A. The causes of a problem in society
   B. The effects of a societal trend
   C. The effects of a problem in society

Questions 2-4 refer to the following three simplified sentences (from paragraph 2 of both model answers).

> i. **These communication tools help us to keep in touch with people in other countries.**
> ii. **E-mail and chat programs like MSN Messenger are especially useful.**
> iii. **The Internet certainly makes it easier to communicate.**

2. Put the above sentences in the correct order.

   A. ii. / i. / iii.
   B. i. / ii. / iii.
   C. iii. / ii. / i.

3. Which of these sentences is the most general?

   A. i.
   B. ii.
   C. iii.

4. What does the phrase "***these communication tools***" (see Model Answer A) refer to?

   A. e-mail and chat programs like MSN Messenger
   B. the Internet
   C. people in other countries

5. What verb tenses does the writer use in these essays?
   A. past and present tense
   B. past tense
   C. past, present perfect and present tense

6. Which of the following sentences is grammatically correct (see Model Answer B)?
   A. The Internet has brought significant changes to our lives in recent years.
   B. The Internet has brought significant changes to our life in recently.
   C. The Internet brought significant changes to our lives in recent years.

7. Which of the following sentences is grammatically correct (see Model Answer A)?
   A. In the past, research had involved spending many hours in the library.
   B. In the past, research has involved spending many hours in the library.
   C. In the past, research involved spending many hours in the library.

Answer these questions by writing YES or NO

8. The writer says what other people think before offering his own opinion (see Model Answer A).

9. In Model Answer B, the word "***benefit***" is used as both a noun and a verb.

10. In Model Answer B, "***pornography***" is an example of "***offensive or dangerous material***".

Check your answers

1. **B**

The Internet has advantages and disadvantages, so it is a trend not a problem.

2. **C**

The first sentence (iii.) says that the Internet makes it easier to communicate; the second (ii.) gives examples of internet communication; and the last sentence (i.) says how these programs help us.

3. **C**

You should start each paragraph with a general sentence and then give specific examples to support it.

4. **A**

5. **C**

Any time you need to talk about changes between the past and the present, you will probably need these three tenses.

6. **A**

Any time you write "***recently***" or "***in recent times***", you will probably need to use present perfect tense (has/have done). Also, the plural form of "***life***" is "***lives***".

7. **C**

Whenever you write "***in the past***" or "***in earlier times***", you will probably need to use past tense.

8. **YES**

This makes the writer's opinion seem stronger.

9. **YES**

"***Benefit***" can be a noun or a verb. The adjective is "***beneficial***".

10. **YES**

Question 12 Fast Food 快餐

WRITING TASK 2

You should spend about 40 minutes on this task.

Write about the following topic:

> ***Fast food is now universally available in most countries and is becoming increasingly popular. Some feel that this is a positive trend, while others do not.***
>
> ***What are your opinions on this?***

Give reasons for your answer and include any relevant examples from your own knowledge or experience.

Write at least 250 words.

Model Answer A: IELTS Band 5^+

There are various different perspectives on the issue of fast food. Some people believe that this kind of food has a positive role to play in the world because of its convenience and low cost; however, I would argue that it is harmful both to the people who eat it and to society at large. There are two main reasons for this.

Firstly, it is a well-known fact that eating too much fast food is extremely unhealthy. Foods such as fried chicken, hamburgers and chips contain a great deal of fat and salt, which cause major health problems like high blood pressure, obesity and heart disease. Although I certainly agree that fast food is both cheap and convenient, the illnesses it causes when we get older are very expensive and it is the taxpayer who often has to pay for this treatment.

In addition to this, many fast food restaurants advertise to children in order to influence their future eating habits. The McDonalds clown is a good example of this kind of advertising. Ronald McDonald's bright clothes and smile are clearly designed to attract the attention of children, who then push their parents to take them to McDonalds. I believe the restaurant does this because it feels that children who grow up eating in McDonalds are likely to become lifelong customers. Interestingly, McDonalds also provides playgrounds and holds children's birthday parties to get busy parents through the door.

In conclusion, I once again restate my view that fast food has a negative effect on our lives because of the health problems it causes and the way that fast food chains try to change the eating habits of children.

(278 words)

Model Answer B: IELTS Band 7+

The past 50 years have seen a dramatic increase in the availability of fast food. Some laud its convenience and relatively low cost; however, in this essay I intend to argue that this kind of food is detrimental both to the individuals that consume it and to society at large. There are two primary reasons for this.

First of all, it is an undeniable fact that consuming fast food to excess results in serious health problems. Foods such as fried chicken, hamburgers and chips—which are incredibly high in fat and salt—are responsible for such ailments as high blood pressure, obesity and heart disease. Moreover, although I certainly agree that fast food is both affordable and convenient, the cost and inconvenience of treating the illnesses it causes in later life are significant. In other words, while fast food is beneficial in the short term, its long-term effects are generally negative.

Further and even more importantly, though, some fast food chains deliberately attempt to attract children in order to shape their future eating habits. One particularly good example of this is the character Ronald McDonald—the bright clothes and smile of the McDonalds clown are a beacon to children. Having grown up eating in McDonalds restaurants, people are likely to continue eating there throughout their adult lives. It is also interesting to note that McDonalds provides playgrounds and frequently holds children's birthday parties in order to attract young children and their parents.

By way of conclusion, I believe that fast food will continue to become more popular as the pace of life increases. Given the health risks associated with this trend, I believe that public education campaigns warning people about the dangers of fast food would be warranted.

(288 words)

Model Sentence Structures 句型示范

Sentence 1	IELTS 5	Fast food is now much more widely available than it was 50 years ago.
	IELTS 6	In the past 50 years the availability of fast food has increased dramatically.
	IELTS 7+	The past 50 years have seen a dramatic increase in the availability of fast food.
Sentence 2	IELTS 6	Some people feel that this kind of food plays a positive role in the world because it is convenient and cheap.
	IELTS 7+	Some people believe that this kind of food has a positive role to play in the world because of its convenience and low cost.
Sentence 3	IELTS 5	But I believe that this kind of food is bad for the people who eat it and also for society.
	IELTS 6	However, in this essay I will argue that this kind of food is harmful both to the individuals who eat it and to society in general.
	IELTS 7+	However, in this essay I intend to argue that this kind of food is detrimental both to the individuals that consume it and to society at large.
Sentence 4	IELTS 5	As everybody knows, fast food is very unhealthy.
	IELTS 6	Firstly, it is a well-known fact that eating too much fast food causes serious health problems.
	IELTS 7+	First of all, it is an undeniable fact that eating fast food to excess results in serious health problems.

Sentence 5	**IELTS 5**	Foods like fried chicken, hamburgers and chips contain large amounts of fat and salt. They cause illnesses like high blood pressure, weight problems and heart disease.
	IELTS 6	Foods such as fried chicken, hamburgers and chips are very high in fat and salt. These foods are responsible for ailments like high blood pressure, obesity and heart disease.
	IELTS 7⁺	Foods such as fried chicken, hamburgers and chips—which are incredibly high in fat and salt—are responsible for such ailments as high blood pressure, obesity and heart disease.

Academic Vocabulary 高分词汇

Basic 基础 5+分	Intermediate 中级 6+分	Advanced 高级 7+分
	cause (n./v.)	(be) responsible for/ result in
	harmful (adj.)	detrimental (adj.)
	firstly (adv.) first of all	
too much		to excess
		(be) incredibly high in fat/ contain a great deal of fat
	illness (n.)	ailment (n.)
	serious health problem	major health problem
	when we get older	in later life
	although (conj.) while (conj.)	
cheap (adj.)		affordable (adj.)
	in addition to this	further and even more importantly, though, ...
	believe (v.) feel (v.)	
	interestingly (adv.)	it is interesting to note that
eat (v.)		consume (v.)
	in conclusion	by way of conclusion
	danger (n.)	risk (n.)

Test Your Comprehension 综合练习

Answer these questions by circling A, B or C

1. Question 12 asks you to write about:
   A. the effects of a societal problem
   B. the causes of a problem in society
   C. the positive and negative effects of a societal trend

2. Choose the best title for these two essays.
   A. Fast food is a bad thing.
   B. Fast food is a good thing.
   C. Fast food is unhealthy.

3. Choose the best summary of Model Answer B.
   A. We should warn people about the dangers of fast food. It is unhealthy and fast food chains try to change children's eating habits. Fast food is a bad thing.
   B. Fast food is a bad thing. It is unhealthy and fast food chains try to change children's eating habits. We should warn people about the dangers of fast food.
   C. Fast food is unhealthy and fast food chains try to change children's eating habits. Fast food is a bad thing. We should warn people about the dangers of fast food.

4. In Model Answer B, the word "***laud***" means:
   A. dislike
   B. discuss
   C. welcome

5. Which of the following statements is grammatically correct?
   A. This kind of foods have a positive role to play in the world because it is convenience.
   B. This kind of food has a positive role to play in the world because of it is convenient.
   C. This kind of food has a positive role to play in the world because of its convenience.

6. In paragraph 2 of both model answers, "***obesity***" means:
   A. fatness
   B. overeating
   C. fat

7. In the phrase "***having grown up eating in McDonalds restaurants***" (see Model Answer B) the word "***having***" means:
   A. before
   B. after
   C. during

Answer these questions by writing YES or NO

8. In these essays, the writer says that the growing popularity of fast food is a positive trend.

9. "***Because of***" (see Model Answer A) is exactly the same as "***given***" (see Model Answer B).

10. In Model Answer B, the writer uses the word "***moreover***" in the middle of a paragraph.

11. "***A great deal of***" (see Model Answer A) means "***a little***".

12. The writer makes a suggestion in the conclusion of Model Answer B.

Check your answers

1. **C**
"***Societal trend***" means "***trend in society***".

2. **A**
The writer says this at the end of paragraph 1 using different words: "***It (fast food) is harmful both to the people who eat it and to society at large***". You should always state your opinion at the end of your introduction.

3. **B**
You should plan your essay by writing this kind of summary on a separate piece of paper before you start writing the actual essay.

4. **C**
"***Laud***" means to "***like***" and "***welcome***" a new trend or development.

5. **C**
"***Because of***" must be followed by a noun such as "***convenience***".

6. **A**
"***Fatness***" is not a real word in English. You must write "***obesity***" instead.

7. **B**

8. **NO**
The writer says that the popularity of fast food is a negative trend.

9. **YES**
Look at question 5 (above) to see how to use "***because of***".

10. **YES**
The writer uses this word in the middle of the paragraph to make a stronger point on the same topic. This is the best place for it.

11. **NO**
It means "***a lot***".

12. **YES**
This is often a good way to conclude.

Question 13 International Tourism 国际旅行

WRITING TASK 2

You should spend about 40 minutes on this task.

Write about the following topic:

> ***International tourism is now more common than ever before. Some feel that this is a positive trend, while others do not.***
>
> ***What are your opinions on this?***

Give reasons for your answer and include any relevant examples from your own knowledge or experience.

Write at least 250 words.

Model Answer A: IELTS Band 5^+

International tourism has increased considerably in the last 50 years. While this industry has certainly created a great deal of wealth for many destination countries, I believe that it has actually caused far more problems than it has solved. The following are just two of the main difficulties involved with international tourism.

One particularly serious issue is that international travel has brought western problems to developing countries. Only wealthy people can afford to travel overseas. As a result, increasing numbers of tourists from rich (mostly western) countries now holiday in poorer countries like Thailand and Indonesia. In many of these places, this flood of tourists is closely associated with such problems as prostitution, alcoholism and drug abuse. Although international tourism can certainly bring people together and create greater cross-cultural understanding, this will probably not happen while it is still such a powerful sign of western power and lack of moral standards.

Even more worrying, however, is the damage that international tourism has caused to the environment in many parts of the world. Australia's Great Barrier Reef is an especially good example of this—large areas of coral reef have been slowly destroyed by the thousands of boats, scuba divers and snorkellers that have visited it over the years. Likewise, Bali's famous Kuta Beach is now often covered in litter from the crowds who go there. In order to maintain such tourist attractions, I feel we must regulate international tourism more carefully.

To conclude, it is clear that the difficulties created by the growing international tourist trade are complicated and many. While they are certainly not impossible to overcome, I believe these problems will probably continue for some time.

(278 words)

Model Answer B: IELTS Band 7⁺

The past 50 years have seen a considerable increase in global tourism. Despite the undeniable economic prosperity it has brought to many host countries, I would argue that the overall impact of international holidaymaking has in fact been negative. Two of the primary drawbacks associated with this trend are as follows.

First of all, global tourism tends to export many negative aspects of western culture. Since it is only the wealthy who can afford to travel abroad, developing countries like Thailand and Indonesia have become the playgrounds of tourists from more affluent ones. In many such nations, this influx of mainly western tourists has brought with it problems such as prostitution as well as alcoholism and drug abuse. Admittedly, international tourism does have the potential to foster greater understanding and tolerance between people of different cultures. However, this is unlikely to occur while it remains such a potent symbol of western cultural domination and moral decadence.

Even more disturbing, though, is the environmental degradation that international tourism has caused in many parts of the world. One particularly salient example of this is the Great Barrier Reef in Australia—the countless boats, divers and snorkellers that have visited the reef over the past few decades have gradually destroyed vast sections of coral. Similarly, world renowned Kuta Beach in Bali has become heavily polluted in recent years. In order to be sustainable, greater regulation of global tourism is required.

In conclusion, the challenges presented by the booming international tourist industry are numerous and complex. Although they are by no means insurmountable, it is highly unlikely that they will be resolved in the foreseeable future.

(272 words)

Model Sentence Structures 句型示范

Sentence 1	IELTS 5	I will now discuss two of the main problems caused by international tourism.
	IELTS 6	The following are just two of the main difficulties involved with international tourism.
	IELTS 7+	Two of the primary drawbacks associated with this trend are as follows.
Sentence 2	IELTS 5	Because only rich people have enough money to travel overseas, poorer countries like Thailand and Indonesia have become the playgrounds of richer ones.
	IELTS 6	As it is only the rich that can afford to holiday overseas, poorer countries such as Thailand and Indonesia have become the playgrounds of wealthier nations.
	IELTS 7+	Since it is only the wealthy who can afford to travel abroad, developing countries like Thailand and Indonesia have become the playgrounds of tourists from more affluent ones.
Sentence 3	IELTS 5	In many of these countries, this increasing number of visitors (mostly from western countries) has caused problems like prostitution, alcoholism and drug abuse.
	IELTS 6	In many such countries, this flood of mostly western tourists has created problems like prostitution along with alcoholism and drug abuse.
	IELTS 7+	In many such nations, this influx of mainly western tourists has brought with it problems such as prostitution as well as alcoholism and drug abuse.

Sentence 4	IELTS 5	However, the damage that global tourism has caused to the environment in many places is even more worrying.
	IELTS 6	Even more worrying, however, is the damage that international tourism has caused to the environment in many parts of the world.
	IELTS 7^+	Even more disturbing, though, is the environmental degradation that international tourism has caused in many parts of the world.
Sentence 5	IELTS 5	Australia's Great Barrier Reef is an especially good example of this—large areas of coral reef have been slowly destroyed by the thousands of boats, scuba divers and snorkellers that have visited it over the years.
	IELTS 6	One especially good example of this is Australia's Great Barrier Reef—the numerous boats, divers and snorkellers who have been there in recent years have slowly destroyed large areas of coral reef.
	IELTS 7^+	One particularly salient example of this is the Great Barrier Reef in Australia—the countless boats, divers and snorkellers that have visited the reef over the past few decades have gradually destroyed vast sections of coral.
Sentence 6	IELTS 5	They are certainly not impossible to overcome, but I believe these problems will probably continue for some time.
	IELTS 6	They are certainly not insurmountable; however, it is very unlikely that they will be solved in the near future.
	IELTS 7^+	Although they are by no means insurmountable, it is highly unlikely that they will be resolved in the foreseeable future.

Academic Vocabulary 高分词汇

Basic 基础 5+分	Intermediate 中级 6+分	Advanced 高级 7+分
last (adj.)	past (adj.)	
international (adj.)	global (adj.)	
	although (conj.) while (conj.)	
	industry (n.) trade (n.)	
	wealth (n.)	prosperity (n.)
country (n.)	nation (n.)	
	destination country/ host country	
travel (n.)	tourism (n.)	holidaymaking (n.)
actually (adv.)	in fact	
	bring problems/ cause problems	create difficulties
	create wealth	bring economic prosperity
solve (v.)	resolve (v.)	
main (adj.)		primary (adj.)
many (adj.)	numerous (adj.)	countless (adj.)
problem (n.)	difficulty (n.)	challenge (n.)
	involved with	associated with
rich (adj.)	wealthy (adj.)	affluent (adj.)
overseas (adj./adv.)	abroad (adj./adv.)	
visit (v.)	holiday in	
poorer country	developing country	
like (conj.) such as		
flood (n.)		influx (n.)

Basic 基础	Intermediate 中级	Advanced 高级
	mostly (adv.)	mainly (adv.)
and (conj.)	as well as	
	not likely	highly unlikely
powerful (adj.)		potent (adj.)
sign (n.)		symbol (n.)
power (n.)		domination (n.)
	lack of moral standards	moral decadence
	worrying (adj.)	disturbing (adj.)
	however (conj.) though (conj.)	
	damage (n.)	degradation (n.)
	especially (adv.)	particularly (adv.)
good example		salient example
	large (adj.)	vast (adj.)
slowly (adv.)	gradually (adv.)	
area (n.)	section (n.)	
	likewise (adv.) similarly (adv.)	
famous (adj.)		world renowned
	in recent years	over the past few decades
growing (adj.)		booming (adj.)
complicated (adj.)	complex (adj.)	
	certainly not	by no means
	impossible to overcome	insurmountable (adj.)

Test Your Comprehension 综合练习

Answer these questions by circling A, B or C

1. Question 13 asks you to:
   A. say why tourism is a negative trend
   B. discuss how travel affects holidaymakers
   C. agree or disagree that tourism is a negative trend and give reasons for your view

Questions 2-4 refer to the following three simplified sentences (taken from Model Answer B).

> **i. The countries these tourists visit include Indonesia and Thailand.**
> **ii. Rich western tourists bring certain problems to the places they visit.**
> **iii. The problems they bring include drug abuse, alcoholism and prostitution.**

2. Put the above sentences in the correct order.
   A. iii. / ii. / i.
   B. ii. / i. / iii.
   C. i. / ii. / iii.

3. Which of the above sentences gives examples of less affluent nations?
   A. i.
   B. ii.
   C. iii.

4. Which of the above sentences is the topic sentence (the most general sentence)?
   A.i.
   B. ii.
   C. iii.

5. Which of the following statements is grammatically wrong?
   A. People in some places believe that western tourists lack moral standards.
   B. People in some places believe that western tourists lack of moral standards.
   C. There is a lack of moral standards among some western tourists.

6. In Model Answer B, "***is unlikely to***" means:
   A. will probably not
   B. might
   C. will probably

Answer these questions by writing YES or NO

7. The word "***insurmountable***" (see Model Answer B) means "***cannot be overcome***".

8. In the introduction to Model Answer B, the writer says that tourism has made many countries richer.

9. In Model Answer B, the writer says that international tourism has damaged the environment.

10. The phrase "***as a result***" (see Model Answer A) is a more formal (and better) way to say "***so***".

Check your answers

1. **C**

2. **B**

   Note that the sentences become progressively more specific.

3. **A**

   "***Thailand***" and "***Indonesia***" are examples of poorer (less affluent) countries.

4. **B**

5. **B**

   "***Lack***" can be a verb or a noun. In the phrase "***a lack of***" the word "***lack***" is a noun. You could write, "***They lack moral standards***" or "***There is a lack of moral standards among these people***".

6. **A**

7. **YES**

8. **YES**

   The writer says that global tourism has brought "***economic prosperity***" to many countries.

9. **YES**

   "***Environmental degradation***" means "***environmental damage***".

10. **YES**

Do You Agree or Disagree?

你同不同意?

Question 14 Immigration
移民

WRITING TASK 2

You should spend about 40 minutes on this task.

Write about the following topic:

> ***Nowadays, more people are migrating to other countries than ever before. In order to become integrated into society in their adopted countries, immigrants should abandon their old ways and adapt to local customs and codes of behaviour.***
>
> ***Do you agree or disagree?***

Give reasons for your answer and include any relevant examples from your own knowledge or experience.

Write at least 250 words.

Model Answer A: IELTS Band 5+

There are a variety of different opinions on whether or not immigrants should change their behaviour to fit in with their new country. Although some people would no doubt disagree, I personally believe that newcomers should indeed try to adapt. In my view, this means following both the written laws and social customs of their adopted country. There are two primary reasons for this.

Firstly, it is obvious that society would not function properly if newcomers did not obey the law. One particularly good example of this is road rules—imagine what would happen if people refused to drive on the same side of the road. Thus, it is necessary for immigrants to make sure that they obey the law in their new country even if laws in their home country are different. Two other examples of things which are allowed in some countries but illegal in others are owning a gun and gambling.

Secondly, it is important to remember that societies are built on shared values. The social rules of a country are the glue that keeps it together, so new immigrants must respect them. Certainly, having many different cultures makes a country more interesting; however, I would argue that too much difference weakens a society by making people feel that they do not belong there. I believe that similarities between people bring them together, while their differences pull them apart. A healthy society is a society with a strong sense of unity.

In conclusion, I once again restate my belief that new immigrants to a country must try to adjust to local rules of behaviour. As the old saying goes: "When in Rome, do as the Romans do".

(280 words)

Model Answer B: IELTS Band 7^{+}

These days, it seems that more people are migrating to other countries than ever before. This raises certain questions about the integration of newcomers into society. Although there are valid arguments to the contrary, in this paper I will argue that it is the responsibility of immigrants to adapt to accepted rules of behaviour in their adopted country, both written and unwritten. The reasons for this are twofold.

Firstly, it is vitally important that newcomers observe the laws of their adopted country for the sake of social order. Imagine the chaos that would ensue if people refused to drive on the same side of the road. It is, therefore, necessary for all immigrants to ensure that they observe the law in their new country regardless of any differences to laws in their home country. Two further instances of practices which are permitted in some countries but prohibited in others are the possession of firearms and gambling.

Secondly and more importantly, though, in order to maintain societal cohesion it is essential that newcomers respect the social norms of their adopted country. Of course, having a mixture of different cultures and traditions gives a country colour and vibrancy; however, I would contend that too much cultural diversity undermines a society by alienating people from each other. It is my belief that similarities unite people, whereas differences have a tendency to divide. A strong society is a homogenous society with shared values and goals.

By way of conclusion, I believe that this issue is likely to become even more important in the future as borders between countries become increasingly blurred. It, therefore, demands our further consideration.

(273 words)

Model Sentence Structures 句型示范

Sentence 1	IELTS 5	First, if we want society to run smoothly, immigrants must follow the rules of their new country.
	IELTS 6	Firstly, it is very important that immigrants obey the laws of their new country to maintain order in society.
	IELTS 7+	Firstly, it is vitally important that newcomers observe the laws of their adopted country for the sake of social order.
Sentence 2	IELTS 5	So immigrants should follow the rules in their new country even if laws in their home country are different.
	IELTS 6	Therefore, immigrants need to make sure that they obey the law in their new country despite any differences to laws in their home country.
	IELTS 7+	It is, therefore, necessary for all immigrants to ensure that they obey the law in their new country regardless of any differences to laws in their home country.
Sentence 3	IELTS 5	It is true that different cultures make a country more interesting, but I believe that too much difference makes it weak by making people feel that they do not fit in there.
	IELTS 6	Certainly, having many cultures makes a country more interesting; however, I would argue that too much difference weakens a society by making people feel that they do not belong there.
	IELTS 7+	Of course, having a mixture of different cultures and traditions gives a country colour and vibrancy; however, I would contend that too much cultural diversity undermines a society by alienating people from each other.

Sentence 4	IELTS 5	I believe that things we have in common bring us together, but differences pull us apart.
	IELTS 6	I believe that similarities between people unite them, while their differences divide them.
	IELTS 7^+	It is my belief that similarities unite people, whereas differences have a tendency to divide.
Sentence 5	IELTS 5	To conclude, I think this question will be even more important in the future because the lines between countries are slowly disappearing.
	IELTS 6	In conclusion, I believe that this issue will probably become even more important in the future as borders between countries become less and less clear.
	IELTS 7^+	By way of conclusion, I believe that this issue is likely to become even more important in the future as borders between countries become increasingly blurred.

Academic Vocabulary 高分词汇

Basic 基础 5+分	Intermediate 中级 6+分	Advanced 高级 7+分
	immigrant (n.) newcomer (n.)	
rule of behaviour/ social rule	social custom	social norm
fit in		adapt (v.) adjust (v.)
new country		adopted country
rule (n.)	law (n.)	
	obey the law	observe the law
	therefore (adv.)	thus (adv.)
important (adj.)	necessary (adj.)	essential (adj.) vitally important
make sure		ensure (v.)
example (n.)		instance (n.)
	allow (v.)	permit (v.)
	illegal (adj.)	prohibited (adj.)
own (v.)		possess (v.)
gun (n.)		firearm (n.)
	social (adj.)	societal (adj.)
	bring together	unite (v.)
	in conclusion	by way of conclusion

Test Your Comprehension 综合练习

Answer these questions by circling A, B or C

1. Choose the best heading for these essays.
   A. Immigrants should drive on the same side of the road as locals.
   B. Newcomers should try to adapt to local ways.
   C. Immigrants should observe the social rules of their adopted country.

2. Choose the best summary for Model Answer B.
   A. Immigrants should try to fit in. Society needs written laws. It also needs social rules. This issue will become even more important in the future.
   B. This issue will become even more important in the future. Society needs social rules. It also needs written laws. Immigrants should try to fit in.
   C. Society needs written laws. It also needs social rules. This issue will become even more important in the future. Immigrants should try to fit in.

3. Which of these is the strongest?
   A. should
   B. must
   C. have to

4. Which of the following sentences is grammatically wrong (see both model answers)?
   A. Imagine the chaos that would ensue if people refused to drive on the same side of the road.
   B. Image the problems it would cause if people refused to drive on the same side of the road.
   C. Imagine what would happen if people refused to drive on the same side of the road.

5. The word "***chaos***" (see Model Answer B) is:
   A. a verb
   B. an adjective
   C. a noun

Answer these questions by writing YES or NO

6. "***Imagine what would happen***" (see Model Answer A) is exactly the same as "***imagine what will happen***".

7. The writer concludes Model Answer A with the English proverb, "***When in Rome, do as the Romans do***". You can also use Chinese proverbs in your essays.

8. The word "***whereas***" (see Model Answer B) is similar to "***but***".

9. The noun "***homogenous***" (see Model Answer B) means "***all the same kind***".

10. "***Increasingly blurred***" (see Model Answer B) means "***less and less clear***".

Check your answers

1. **B**

This means that immigrants should change and try to fit in with local customs.

2. **A**

You should write this kind of summary as a plan before you write your essay. Each sentence in the summary represents one paragraph in your essay.

3. **C**

"***Should***" is used to suggest; "***must***" is used to make a strong suggestion; and "***have to***" is used to talk about an obligation (something you have no choice in) or give an order.

4. **B**

"***Image***" is not a verb; it is a noun that means "***picture***". "***Imagine***" is a verb, so it is correct in these sentences.

5. **C**

"***Chaos***" is a noun; "***chaotic***" is the adjective. There is no verb.

6. **NO**

The first phrase is used to talk about an unreal or imaginary situation; the second one is used to talk about a planned situation.

7. **NO**

Chinese sayings often sound strange in English.

8. **YES**

"***Whereas***" means "***while***" or "***on the other hand***".

9. **NO**

"***Homogenous***" means "***all the same kind***", but it is an adjective.

10. **YES**

Question 15 Jobs and Gender 职业与性别

WRITING TASK 2

You should spend about 40 minutes on this task.

Write about the following topic:

Men and women are different in terms of their characteristics and abilities. For this reason, some jobs are better done by men and others by women.

Do you agree or disagree?

Give reasons for your answer and include any relevant examples from your own knowledge or experience.

Write at least 250 words.

Model Answer A: IELTS Band 5^+

There are a variety of different perspectives on the question of whether or not men and women are equally good at all jobs. Although many people still believe that some kinds of work should only be done by females and other kinds by males, it is my argument that both men and women are able to do any job well. There are two main reasons for this.

Firstly, I would argue that traditional ideas about men and women are not always right. It is certainly true that there are characteristics that are typically male and others which are typically female; however, not everybody is typical. Not every woman is physically weak, in the same way that not every man is a poor communicator—traditional gender roles do not fit everybody. A man who wants to do a job normally performed by women or a woman who wants to work in a male-dominated industry should be given the chance to demonstrate his/her ability.

Furthermore, I feel that having both male and female employees in a workplace creates a sense of balance. The two sexes often, though certainly not always, do things differently. Instead of seeing these differences as weaknesses, I believe that we should view them as chances to find new ways of doing things and thus improve the way we work. Therefore, a person's weak points can be turned into strengths.

To conclude, for the reasons stated above I maintain that men and women can do any job equally well and that a person's individual ability is far more important than their sex in this regard.

(266 words)

Model Answer B: IELTS Band 7+

These days, it seems that more women are entering "male occupations" than ever before and vice versa. While some still hold to the conservative view that certain jobs are better performed by men and others by women, it is my personal belief that people of either sex are capable of doing any job effectively. The reasons for my position are as follows.

First of all, I believe it is a mistake to base our views on broad generalisations about the characteristics of men and women as such stereotypes are often inaccurate. Although there are certainly traits which are typical of men and others which are typical of women, there are exceptions to every rule. Not all women are physically weak, just as not all men are poor interpersonal communicators; conventional gender roles are not appropriate for everybody. If a man or woman desires to pursue a career which is traditionally reserved for the opposite sex, I believe he/she should be provided the opportunity to prove him/herself capable.

Secondly, I would contend that the presence of both males and females in a workplace brings a sense of balance. Men and women frequently, though by no means always, have different methods of doing things. Rather than judging these differences to be weaknesses, I feel that we should view them as opportunities for innovation and the discovery of more effective and efficient work practices. A person's weaknesses can thus be transformed into strengths.

In summary, I once again reaffirm my position that both male and female employees are an asset to any industry and as our stereotypes about men and women are not always appropriate, we must not discourage anyone from choosing an occupation simply because of his/her gender.

(285 words)

Model Sentence Structures 句型示范

Sentence 1	IELTS 5	There are many different opinions about whether or not men and women are equally good at all jobs.
	IELTS 6	There are various different opinions on the question of whether men and women are equally good at all jobs or not.
	IELTS 7+	There are a variety of different perspectives on the question of whether or not men and women are equally good at all jobs.
Sentence 2	IELTS 5	Some people with more traditional views think that women should do some jobs and men should do others, but I believe that both men and women can do any job well.
	IELTS 6	Some people still take the traditional view that some occupations are better done by women and others by men; however, I personally believe that people of either sex are able to do any job effectively.
	IELTS 7+	While some still hold to the conservative view that certain jobs are better performed by men and others by women, it is my personal belief that people of either sex are capable of doing any job effectively.

Sentence 3	IELTS 5	First, we should not base our opinions on traditional ideas about men and women because these ideas are often wrong.
	IELTS 6	First, I feel it is a mistake to base our opinions on broad generalisations about men and women because these stereotypes are often wrong.
	IELTS 7+	First of all, I believe it is a mistake to base our views on broad generalisations about the characteristics of men and women as such stereotypes are often inaccurate.
Sentence 4	IELTS 6	If a man wants to do a job which is usually done by women or if a woman wants to do a man's job, I think he/she should be given the chance to show that he/she can do it.
	IELTS 7+	If a woman desires to pursue a career which is traditionally reserved for the opposite sex or vice versa, I believe he/she should be provided the opportunity to prove him/herself capable.
Sentence 5	IELTS 5	Instead of seeing these differences as weaknesses, I believe we should see them as chances to find new and better ways to work.
	IELTS 6	Instead of judging these differences to be weaknesses, I feel we should view them as opportunities to innovate and discover more effective and efficient ways to work.
	IELTS 7+	Rather than judging these differences to be weaknesses, I feel that we should view them as opportunities for innovation and the discovery of more effective and efficient work practices.

Academic Vocabulary 高分词汇

Basic 基础 5+分	Intermediate 中级 6分	Advanced 高级 7+分
	view (n.) position (n.)	perspective (n.)
	(be) able to	(be) capable of
man (n.)	male (n./adj.)	
woman (n.)	female (n./adj.)	
job (n.)		occupation (n.)
traditional (adj.)		conservative (adj.) conventional (adj.)
	well (adv.)	effectively (adv.)
		although (conj.) while (conj.)
	believe (v.) feel (v.)	
	argue (v.)	contend (v.)
	I believe/ I feel	I would argue/ I would contend
		generalisation (n.) stereotype (n.)
right (adj.)		accurate (adj.)
*sex (n.)		gender (n.)
give (v.)	provide (v.)	
chance (n.)		opportunity (n.)
	bring (v.) create (v.)	
often (adv.)		frequently (adv.)
	instead of	rather than
see (v.)	view (v.)	

Basic 基础 5+分	Intermediate 中级 6分	Advanced 高级 7分
	weak point weakness (n.)	
want (v.)		desire (v.)
	therefore (adv.)	thus (adv.)
		maintain (v.) reaffirm (v.)
	in summary/ to conclude	

Note: The words "sex" and "gender" do not mean exactly the same thing, but the difference between them is very small and for IELTS purposes they can be used interchangeably.

Test Your Comprehension 综合练习

Answer these questions by circling A, B or C

1. Question 15 asks you to:
   A. list the different characteristics of men and women
   B. say why men are such poor communicators
   C. agree or disagree that men and women can do any job equally well and explain why

Question 2 refers to the following four simplified sentences based on the above essays.

> i. **Not all women are physically weak.**
> ii. **Therefore, I believe that men and women can do any job equally well.**
> iii. **Similarly, not every man is a poor communicator.**
> iv. **Traditional ideas about men and women are not always right because not everybody is typical.**

2. Put the above sentences in the correct order.
   A. iii. / ii. / i. / iv.
   B. iv. / i. / iii. / ii.
   C. i. / ii. / iii. / iv.

3. Which of the following sentences is wrong (see Model Answer B)?
   A. If a person desires to pursue a career which is traditionally reserved for the opposite sex, I believe they should be provided the opportunity to prove themselves capable.
   B. If a man or woman desires to pursue a career which is traditionally reserved for the opposite sex, I believe he/she should be provided the opportunity to prove him/herself capable.
   C. If a man or woman desires to pursue a career which is traditionally reserved for the opposite sex, I believe he should be provided the opportunity to prove himself capable.

4. Which of the following means "***I still believe***" (see Model Answer A)?
   A. I maintain
   B. I would contend
   C. I feel

5. What two stereotypes are mentioned in these essays?
   A. Women are weak and men do not know how to communicate with people.
   B. Men are physically strong and know how to communicate with people.
   C. Women are good with children, while men are good at earning money.

Answer these questions by writing YES or NO

6. The main reason that Model Answer B would get a higher IELTS band score is because it is longer than Model Answer A.

7. "***Certain jobs***" (see Model Answer B) is a better way to say "***some jobs***" because it is more formal.

8. "***Simply***" (see Model Answer B) is a more formal way to say "***only***".

9. The writer gives several examples of jobs that women should not do.

Check your answers

1. **C**
You must agree or disagree with the statement (in your introduction) and give reasons (in the main body of your essay).

2. **B**
The writer says that stereotypes are not always right, gives two examples of inaccurate stereotypes, and then concludes.

3. **C**
Nowadays, you cannot just write "***he***" because it is considered sexist. You must try to be inclusive.

4. **A**

5. **A**

6. **NO**
Length is not the most important factor.

7. **YES**
"***Certain***" often means "***some***" and is more academic sounding.

8. **YES**

9. **NO**
Because the writer does not believe that there are any jobs that should only be done by men or women.

Question 16 Cigarette Smoking 吸烟

WRITING TASK 2

You should spend about 40 minutes on this task.

Write about the following topic:

> ***Smoking is a major cause of serious illness and death throughout the world today. In the interest of public health, governments should ban cigarettes and other tobacco products.***
>
> ***Do you agree or disagree?***

Give reasons for your answer and include any relevant examples from your own knowledge or experience.

Write at least 250 words.

Model Answer A: IELTS Band 5+

There are a range of different views on the question of whether tobacco should be banned or not. Some people would argue that smoking is a personal choice and that introducing laws to prevent people from smoking would be repressive. However, I feel that tobacco should indeed be made illegal. There are two main reasons for this.

Firstly, it is important to remember that tobacco is actually a drug. Most countries around the world have strict laws against selling or using recreational drugs. Therefore, if governments want to be consistent in the way they handle the problem of drug abuse, I believe they must ban tobacco as well. This is especially true considering the fact that many drugs which are now illegal, such heroin and marijuana, could be used by doctors to treat various real medical problems. On the other hand, tobacco is useless.

Further and even more importantly, though, smoking should be banned for the sake of public health. It is a proven fact that smoking causes serious illnesses, such as lung cancer and heart disease. Although cigarette companies and pro-smoking groups may claim that people have the right to decide what to put into their own bodies, I would argue that the rights of society are more important than those of the individual. The medical treatment smokers need when they get sick is often very expensive, and it is usually governments and society who pay the bill. Thus, I believe that anti-smoking laws would be a good idea.

To conclude, although governments will probably not ban tobacco in the near future, I feel this should be the long-term goal as there are few habits as pointless and destructive as smoking.

(283 words)

Model Answer B: IELTS Band 7⁺

There are widely differing views on the issue of whether tobacco should be banned or not. Some people would suggest that it is their right to smoke and that prohibiting cigarettes would be a violation of their civil liberties; however, I personally believe that tobacco should indeed be made illegal. There are two principal reasons for this.

One point which I believe to be absolutely pivotal is the fact that tobacco is a drug. The majority of governments around the world take a prohibitionist approach to the problem of substance abuse. If governments wish to be consistent in pursuing their "war on drugs", therefore, I believe they must ban tobacco as well. This is particularly so given the fact that many currently illicit drugs—including heroin and marijuana—have legitimate medical applications, while tobacco has none.

However, perhaps the strongest argument in favour of banning cigarettes and other tobacco products is that of public health. It is an irrefutable fact that smoking leads to lung cancer and other such potentially fatal diseases. Pro-smoking groups would no doubt argue that each individual has the right to determine what goes into his/her own body. Nevertheless, I would suggest that the interests and rights of society at large must override those of the individual. The medical treatment that smokers require is often incredibly costly, and it is frequently governments and society that cover these costs rather than the individual smoker. Hence, I feel that laws prohibiting smoking would be entirely justified.

In reality, of course, the widespread prohibition of smoking is unlikely in the near future. However, given the seriousness of the problems that it causes, I believe that this should be the ultimate goal.

(282 words)

Model Sentence Structures 句型示范

Sentence 1	IELTS 5	One thing that I think is very important is that tobacco is a drug.
	IELTS 6	One thing which I believe to be vitally important is the fact that tobacco is a drug.
	IELTS 7+	One point which I believe to be absolutely pivotal is the fact that tobacco is a drug.
Sentence 2	IELTS 5	This is especially true because doctors could use some illegal drugs, like heroin and marijuana, to treat sick people if they were not banned.
	IELTS 6	This is especially so considering the fact that some drugs which are now illegal, such heroin and marijuana, could be used by doctors to treat various real medical problems.
	IELTS 7+	This is particularly so given the fact that some currently illicit drugs—including heroin and marijuana—have legitimate medical applications, while tobacco has none.
Sentence 3	IELTS 5	But maybe the best reason to ban smoking is that it is bad for our health.
	IELTS 6	However, possibly the best argument for banning cigarettes and other tobacco products is public health.
	IELTS 7+	However, perhaps the strongest argument in favour of banning cigarettes and other tobacco products is that of public health.

Sentence 4	**IELTS 6**	It is a proven fact that smoking causes lung cancer and other serious illnesses.
	IELTS 7⁺	It is an irrefutable fact that smoking leads to lung cancer and other such potentially fatal diseases.
Sentence 5	**IELTS 5**	So I think that there are a number of very good reasons to ban smoking.
	IELTS 6	Thus, I believe it would be justifiable to ban smoking.
	IELTS 7⁺	Hence, I feel that laws prohibiting smoking would be entirely justified.
Sentence 6	**IELTS 5**	Of course, the fact is that smoking probably will not be banned for many years to come.
	IELTS 6	Of course, in reality smoking is unlikely to be prohibited in the near future.
	IELTS 7⁺	In reality, of course, the widespread prohibition of smoking is unlikely in the near future.

Academic Vocabulary 高分词汇

Basic 基础 5+分	Intermediate 中级 6分	Advanced 高级 7+分
question (n./v.)	issue (n.)	
	ban (n./v.)	prohibit (v.)
	illegal (adj.)	illicit (adj.)
main (adj.)		principal (adj.)
important (adj.)		absolutely pivotal
	therefore (adv.)	thus (adv.) hence (adv.)
most (adj.)		the majority of
	drug abuse	substance abuse
want (v.)		wish (v.)
		especially (adv.) particularly (adv.)
	proven (adj.)	irrefutable (adj.)
	cause (n./v.)	lead to
pay the bill		cover the costs
	illness (n.) disease (n.)	
expensive (adj.)		costly (adj.)
decide (v.)		determine (v.)
		I would argue that/ I would suggest that
need (v.)		require (v.)
	however (adv.)	nevertheless (adv.)
very (adv.)	incredibly (adv.)	
often (adv.)	frequently (adv.)	
	feel (v.) believe (v.)	

Test Your Comprehension 综合练习

Answer these questions by circling A, B or C

1. Question 16 is about:
   A. why people like to smoke
   B. how we can stop people from smoking
   C. whether smoking should be banned

Question 2 refers to the following three simplified sentences (from paragraph 1 of both model answers).

i. **Some people believe that they have the right to smoke.** ii. **But I think smoking should be illegal.** iii. **There is little agreement on the issue of banning smoking.**

2. Put the above sentences in the correct order.
   A. ii. / i. / iii.
   B. i. / ii. / iii.
   C. iii. / i. / ii.

3. What reasons does the writer give for banning smoking?
   A. Smoking is unhealthy, but drugs like heroin and marijuana are worse.
   B. Smoking is unhealthy and should be treated in the same way as other drugs.
   C. Smoking is unhealthy and many drugs which are now illegal, such as heroin and marijuana, could be used by doctors.

4. Which of the following sentences is a grammatically correct way to make a prediction about the possible results of an action?
   A. Laws banning smoking would improve public health.
   B. Laws banning smoking will improve public health.
   C. Laws banning smoking have improved public health.

5. Which of the following is the weakest?
   A. have to
   B. must
   C. should

6. Which of the following means "*most*" (see Model Answer B)?
   A. a minority of
   B. the majority of
   C. a large proportion of

Answer these questions by writing YES or NO

7. Most countries will certainly ban smoking in the future.

8. "*Wish to*" (see Model Answer B) is a more formal way to say "*want to*".

9. "*Pro-smoking groups*" (see Model Answer B) refers to people who dislike smoking and want it banned.

10. "*Costly*" (see Model Answer B) means "*cheap*".

Check your answers

1. **C**

2. **C**

One way to start an introduction to this kind of opinion-type essay is to say that people tend to disagree about the topic, then say what other people think, and finally state your opinion. You should not give reasons for your opinion in the introduction.

3. **B**

4. **A**

"***Would***" is correct, because the writer thinks it is unlikely that governments will ban smoking. This kind of sentence structure is common in IELTS Writing Task 2.

5. **C**

"***Should***" is a suggestion, whereas "***must***" is a very strong suggestion and "***have to***" means that there is no choice.

6. **B**

"***The majority of***" is a more formal way to write "***most***".

7. **NO**

What will happen in the future is never 100% certain.

8. **YES**

"***Wish***" has two different meanings. "***Wish to***" means "***want to***" in formal writing (E.g. I wish to enrol in your Master's programme); however, "***wish***" can also mean to want something impossible.

9. **NO**

"***Pro***" means to like and support something. The opposite of "***pro***" is "***anti***".

10. **NO**

"***Costly***" means "***expensive***".

Question 17 Endangered Species
濒临灭绝的生物

WRITING TASK 2

You should spend about 40 minutes on this task.

Write about the following topic:

> ***Trying to save endangered animal species from extinction is a waste of valuable resources.***
>
> ***Do you agree or disagree?***

Give reasons for your answer and include any relevant examples from your own knowledge or experience.

Write at least 250 words.

5+ 分

Model Answer A: IELTS Band 5+

The question of whether or not we should try to save endangered species is definitely a controversial one. Although some people argue that these animals are not useful and that we should let them die out in the same way that many others (like the dinosaurs) have died out before, I personally believe that endangered species are actually worth saving. There are two main reasons for this.

First of all, it is important for us to recognise the key role that endangered species play in nature. The environment is made up of fragile ecosystems, where plants and animals all rely on one another to survive. If one animal disappears or a new one is introduced, it upsets the balance of nature and affects other animals above and below it in the food chain by changing the environment that they live in. These changes often come back to affect us in ways that we do not expect. In the same way that rabbits introduced to Australia by the British now eat the plants that many native animals need to live and ruin farmers' crops, the extinction of a predatory animal would allow its prey to reproduce out of control and would probably cause plagues. Thus, because environmental change is actually a danger to us, we clearly have an interest in saving endangered species.

However, maybe the strongest argument for saving endangered species is that all life is valuable in and of itself. Even if these animals do not have any practical use, they should still be saved. Furthermore, because human activity has destroyed the natural living environment of many endangered species, we should do the best we can to save them.

To conclude, I feel that endangered animal species are indeed worth saving. They not only have their own value, but the balance of nature would be disturbed if they died out.

(311 words)

Model Answer B: IELTS Band 7⁺

The issue of whether we should attempt to save endangered species from extinction or not is certainly a contentious one. Despite the arguments of some people that such animals serve no useful purpose and should be allowed to die out just as many others (including the dinosaurs) have in the past, it is my personal belief that they should in fact be preserved. Two of the principal reasons for this are as follows.

Firstly, it is vital that we appreciate the importance of endangered species in maintaining the balance of nature. Ecosystems are delicate arrangements where plants and animals all depend on each other for survival. The disappearance or introduction of any animal species disrupts the balance and negatively impacts upon other plants and animals by breaking the food chain and altering the habitat in which they live. Such imbalances frequently return to haunt us in unexpected ways. Just as rabbits that were introduced to Australia soon after European settlement now compete with native species for food and destroy farmers' crops, the extinction of a predator can cause plagues by allowing its prey to multiply unchecked. Therefore, since ecological change constitutes a potential risk to us and our environment, it is clearly in our own interests to protect endangered species.

Yet, perhaps the strongest argument in favour of preserving endangered species is that all life has intrinsic value; even if endangered species are not useful to us in any practical way they should be preserved nevertheless. Further, given that we humans are responsible for destroying the natural habitat of many endangered animals, we should make every possible effort to save them.

In conclusion, I once again restate my view that saving endangered species is worthwhile. Not only do they help to maintain the balance of nature, but they also have value in and of themselves.

(305 words)

Model Sentence Structures 句型示范

Sentence 1	IELTS 5	Some people say that we should let these animals die out just like the dinosaurs did because they are not useful, but I think that they should be saved.
	IELTS 6	Although some people might argue that these animals are not useful and should be allowed to die out just like many others (such as the dinosaurs) have died out in the past, I personally believe that they should be saved.
	IELTS 7^+	Despite the arguments of some people that such animals serve no useful purpose and should be allowed to die out just as many others (including the dinosaurs) have in the past, it is my personal belief that they should in fact be preserved.
Sentence 2	IELTS 5	When an animal disappears or a new one is introduced, it disturbs the balance of nature and negatively affects other plants and animals by breaking the food chain and changing their natural environment.
	IELTS 6	When any animal species disappears or a new one is introduced, it disrupts the balance and negatively influences other plants and animals by breaking the food chain and altering the environment which they live in.
	IELTS 7^+	The disappearance or introduction of any animal species disrupts the balance and negatively impacts upon other plants and animals by breaking the food chain and altering the habitat in which they live.

Sentence 3	IELTS 6	Imbalances like this often come back and cause unexpected problems in the future.
	IELTS 7+	Such imbalances frequently return to haunt us in unexpected ways.
Sentence 4	IELTS 5	Clearly, we should save endangered species because environmental change is dangerous to us and also to the world that we live in.
	IELTS 6	Because ecological change is a possible danger to us and to the world that we live in, it is clearly best for us to protect endangered species.
	IELTS 7+	Since ecological change constitutes a potential risk to us and our environment, it is clearly in our own interests to protect endangered species.
Sentence 5	IELTS 5	Also, because we people are destroying the homes of many rare animal species, we should try to save them.
	IELTS 6	Furthermore, since we people are destroying the natural living environment of many endangered animal species, we should make an effort to save them.
	IELTS 7+	Further, given that we humans are responsible for destroying the natural habitat of many endangered animals, we should make every possible effort to save them.

Academic Vocabulary 高分词汇

Basic 基础 5+分	Intermediate 中级 6+分	Advanced 高级 7+分
question (n.)	issue (n.)	
try (v.)		attempt (v.)
save (v.)	protect (v.)	preserve (v.)
	definitely (adv.) certainly (adv.)	
	controversial (adj.)	contentious (adj.)
let (v.)	allow (v.)	
	die out disappear (v.)	become extinct
like (prep.)	including (prep.)	
before (adv.)	in the past	
main (adj.)		principal (adj.)
firstly (adv.) first of all		
important (adj.)		vital (adj.)
	recognise (v.)	appreciate (v.)
		delicate (adj.) fragile (adj.)
	depend on/ rely on	
each other/ one another		
	upset (v.) disturb (v.)	disrupt (v.)
	affect (v.)	impact upon
change (v.)		alter (v.)
often (adv.)	frequently (adv.)	

Basic 基础 5+分	Intermediate 中级 6+分	Advanced 高级 7+分
come back	return (v.)	
	destroy (v.)	ruin (v.)
		predator (n.) predatory animal
	multiply (v.)	reproduce (v.)
out of control		unchecked (adj.)
	therefore (conj.)	thus (conj.)
because (conj.)	since (conj.)	given that
danger (n.)		risk (n.)
maybe (adv.)	perhaps (adv.)	
	still (conj.)	nevertheless (conj.)
	furthermore (conj.)	further (conj.)
natural living environment		habitat (n.)

Test Your Comprehension 综合练习

Answer these questions by circling A, B or C

1. What does Question 17 ask you to do?
   A. say if you think endangered species are worth saving
   B. say why endangered species are dying out
   C. talk about the best way to save endangered species

2. Which of these sentences is the best to use in academic writing (see Model Answer B)?
   A. It's really important for us to save endangered animals.
   B. It is undeniably important that we preserve endangered species.
   C. It's undeniably important that we preserve endangered animal species.

3. Which of the following is not a good sentence to include in your introduction?
   A. Some people would argue that trying to save endangered animal species from extinction is a waste of valuable resources.
   B. Some people would argue that the cost of preventing endangered animals from dying out is too high.
   C. Certainly, preventing endangered animals from becoming extinct is an expensive and difficult endeavour.

4. Which of the following sentences is the most logical?
   A. Some people would suggest that endangered species serve no useful purpose, and I agree that they are not worth saving.
   B. Some people would suggest that saving endangered animals is not worthwhile; however, I believe that such animals should be preserved.
   C. Despite the arguments of some people that endangered animals serve no useful purpose and should be allowed to die out just as many others (including the dinosaurs) have in the past, it is my personal belief that we should not attempt to preserve them.

Answer these questions by writing YES or NO

5. These essays are both too long.

6. The writer argues that endangered species should be saved because they are a vital part of the ecosystems in which they live.

7. The writer suggests that we have a responsibility to preserve endangered animals as we are largely responsible for destroying their homes.

8. The writer repeats his main opinion in the conclusion of both model answers.

Check your answers

1. **A**

2. **B**

Sentence A is too informal; sentence C is not bad, but you should not use contractions (like "***isn't***" or "***can't***") in formal writing.

3. **A**

Sentence A uses exactly the same words as the question. You should try to avoid this.

4. **B**

It sounds strange to write what other people think and then agree with them. You can write your opinion directly without discussing other people's views or write what other people think and then disagree with them.

5. **NO**

There is no maximum word limit. Most candidates should try to write 150-200 words in Task 1 and 250-300 words in Task 2. However, you will not lose marks for writing more. Just make sure you spend enough time on both questions.

6. **YES**

The writer says, "***Firstly, it is vital that we appreciate the importance of endangered species in maintaining the balance of nature. Ecosystems are delicate arrangements where plants and animals all depend on each other for survival***".

7. **YES**

The writer states, "***Further, given that we humans are responsible for destroying the natural habitat of many endangered animals, we should make every possible effort to save them***".

8. **YES**

This is one thing that you can often do to conclude your essay. It is a good idea to use different words, rather than simply repeating yourself though.

Discuss Causes, Effects and/or Solutions

讨论结果、影响或提出解决方法

Question 18 Rural Depopulation

农村人口外流

WRITING TASK 2

You should spend about 40 minutes on this task.

Write about the following topic:

These days, it seems that an increasing number of people are leaving rural areas to live in the city.

Discuss some of the effects of rural depopulation (migration from the country to the city) and suggest some ways in which this trend could be reversed.

Write at least 250 words.

Model Answer A: IELTS Band 5+

Rural depopulation is a very important issue in many parts of the world today. In this essay, I will discuss some of the main effects of this problem and also offer some possible solutions to it.

Firstly, it is clear that migration away from the country negatively affects life in the city. Serious environmental and social problems often occur when cities become overcrowded. Problems such as air, water and noise pollution are now increasingly common in urban areas around the world because there are simply too many people living there. Pollution can make city life very uncomfortable indeed and can even cause illness. Beijing is a very good example of this. Overcrowding in cities can also lead to high unemployment (especially in poorer parts of the world) and crime.

In order to prevent people from moving away from the country and reduce the size of cities, I feel we must make country life more attractive. In my view, the best way of doing this would be to improve services in the country. One of the main reasons that so many people have left the country is that facilities like shopping centres, cinemas, swimming pools, restaurants, libraries, schools and hospitals are generally better in the city. If such facilities were available in the country, more people would choose to live there. Another effective solution would be for the government to subsidise businesses and workers who move to the country.

In conclusion, I believe we must all recognise how serious this problem is. For the sake of the environment and our own quality of life it is vital that we preserve rural communities.

(271 words)

Model Answer B: IELTS Band 7⁺

While country towns were once vibrant and growing places, these days many appear to be dying as people move to the city in search of work and excitement. In this essay, I intend to discuss the impact of this problem as well as how more people could be encouraged to live in rural areas.

Surprisingly, the most serious consequences of rural depopulation are often felt in urban areas. As a result of overcrowding, cities throughout the world today are increasingly prone to environmental problems like air, water and noise pollution. Beijing is a particularly good example of this. Further, the uncontrolled growth of cities also gives rise to social problems such as high unemployment, crime and, in less affluent countries, the creation of slums. Clearly, there is a limit to how many people can live in one area before living standards are negatively influenced.

In order to stem the tide of rural depopulation, I believe we must first address its root causes. At the heart of the matter is the disparity between services and facilities in the country and those in the city. I firmly believe that urban and rural dwellers alike would find the idea of country life far more appealing if high quality shopping centres, cinemas, swimming pools, restaurants, libraries, schools and hospitals were more readily available in the country. One further method of attracting people to the country would be for governments to provide financial incentives to businesses and professional workers who willingly relocate to rural areas.

In reality, this problem is unlikely to be resolved in the short term. However, it is by no means insurmountable, and I am convinced that more people will choose the country life as city life becomes less comfortable and more expensive.

(291 words)

Model Sentence Structures 句型示范

Sentence 1	IELTS 5	It is surprising to note that cities often experience the most serious effects of migration away from the country.
	IELTS 6	It is somewhat surprising that the most serious effects of rural depopulation are often experienced in the city.
	IELTS 7+	Surprisingly, the most serious consequences of rural depopulation are often felt in urban areas.
Sentence 2	IELTS 5	Cities everywhere are having more and more environmental problems like air, water and noise pollution because they are overcrowded.
	IELTS 6	Because of overcrowding, cities around the world today are suffering from more and more environmental problems like air, water and noise pollution.
	IELTS 7+	As a result of overcrowding, cities throughout the world today are increasingly prone to environmental problems like air, water and noise pollution.
Sentence 3	IELTS 5	Overcrowding in cities also causes problems like high unemployment and crime.
	IELTS 6	Further, overcrowding in cities also leads to social problems like high unemployment (especially in poorer parts of the world) and crime.
	IELTS 7+	Further, the uncontrolled growth of cities also gives rise to social problems such as high unemployment, crime and, in less affluent countries, the creation of slums.

Sentence 4	**IELTS 5**	If we want to prevent people from moving to the city we must resolve the causes of the problem.
	IELTS 6	If we are to slow the flow of people moving from the country to the city, I believe we must first resolve its causes.
	IELTS 7⁺	In order to stem the tide of rural depopulation, I believe we must first address its root causes.
Sentence 5	**IELTS 5**	The main cause of the problem is that services and facilities in the country are different from services and facilities in the city.
	IELTS 6	At the centre of the problem is the difference between services and facilities in the country and those in the city.
	IELTS 7⁺	At the heart of the matter is the disparity between services and facilities in the country and those in the city.
Sentence 6	**IELTS 5**	One other way to get people to live in the country would be for governments to give companies and workers money if they move to the country.
	IELTS 6	Another method of attracting people to the country would be for governments to give subsidies to businesses and professional workers who choose to move to the country.
	IELTS 7⁺	One further method of attracting people to the country would be for governments to provide financial incentives to businesses and professional workers who willingly relocate to rural areas.

Academic Vocabulary 高分词汇

Basic 基础 5+分	Intermediate 中级 6分	Advanced 高级 7+分
today (n./adv.)	these days	
affect (v.) effect (n.)	influence (n./v.)	consequence (n.) impact (n./v.)
the country		rural area
the city		urban area
	cause (n./v.)	lead to/ give rise to
poorer (adj.)		less affluent
	feel (v.) believe (v.)	(be) convinced
	resolve (v.)	address (v.)
	attractive (adj.)	appealing (adj.)
		subsidise (v.) provide financial incentives
move (n./v.)		relocate (v.)

Test Your Comprehension 综合练习

Answer these questions by circling A, B or C

1. Question 18 asks you to:
   A. say if you think it is a good or bad thing that people are leaving the country
   B. talk about why people prefer to live in the city and suggest how this trend could be reversed
   C. discuss the consequences of people moving from the country to the city and offer some solutions

2. The writer begins Model Answer B by talking about:
   A. the past
   B. the present
   C. the future

3. The solutions to rural depopulation are strongly connected to:
   A. the city
   B. the effects of the problem
   C. the causes of the problem

4. What negative effects of rural depopulation are mentioned?
   A. pollution, crime and joblessness
   B. pollution and cramped living space
   C. crime, unemployment and high cost of living

Answer these questions by writing YES or NO

5. In the introduction to Model Answer A the writer says what he plans to write about.

6. The writer gives examples of how the problem of rural depopulation affects country towns in both model answers.

7. In both model answers, the writer gives examples of facilities that are better in the city.

8. The word "***increasingly***" (see both model answers) means "***more and more***".

9. In both model answers the writer says that governments should provide more job opportunities in the country.

10. "***Stem the tide***" (see Model Answer B) means "***slow or stop something from happening***".

11. The conclusion of Model Answer B talks about the future of this problem.

Check your answers

1. **C**

The question asks you to discuss the effects (consequences) of the problem and suggest how it could be resolved.

2. **B**

The writer often talks about the past, then talks about the present. This is useful if you need to discuss changes that have happened and say whether you think the past was better or worse than the present.

3. **C**

The best solutions to a problem are usually connected to its causes.

4. **A**

"***Air, water and noise pollution***" are mentioned as well as "***crime***" and "***unemployment***".

5. **YES**

It is a good idea to say what you want to talk about at the end of your introduction.

6. **NO**

The writer gives examples of how rural depopulation affects cities.

7. **YES**

In Model Answer A, the writer states that "***facilities like shopping centres, cinemas, swimming pools, restaurants, libraries, schools and hospitals are generally better in the city***". Model Answer B says something very similar.

8. **YES**

"***Increasingly***" is a better word to use in academic writing. "***More and more***" sounds like spoken English.

9. **NO**

The writer says that governments should "***subsidise businesses and workers who move to the country***". This means that they should give money to these companies and people, not jobs.

10. **YES**

Another way to say the same thing would be "***stem the flow***".

11. **YES**

It is often possible to conclude by talking about the future of a trend or problem.

Question 19 Distance within Modern Families
现代家庭的亲疏关系

WRITING TASK 2

You should spend about 40 minutes on this task.

Write about the following topic:

> ***With divorce rates and family breakdowns increasing globally, it is generally accepted that families today are not as close as they used to be.***
>
> ***Discuss the causes of this problem and offer some possible solutions to it.***

Write at least 250 words.

Model Answer A: IELTS Band 5^+

Lack of communication and closeness between family members is a vitally important issue in many societies today. In this essay, I will firstly discuss the causes of this problem and then offer some possible solutions to it.

In my view, the primary cause of this problem is the modern lifestyle. Most parents today work much harder than ever before. In the past, one parent—usually the mother—stayed at home to take care of the children. In recent times, however, it has become increasingly common for both parents to work. As a result, more and more children now grow up with neither parent at home. It is unsurprising, then, that families are no longer as close as they once were. One other factor adding to this problem is that people today spend too much time on solitary activities like watching television.

In order to overcome this problem and make families closer, people's lifestyles must change. I feel more parents should stay at home and look after their children. Perhaps governments could subsidise parents who choose to look after their families rather than working. Of course, these subsidies would probably not fully cover the income a family would lose if one parent stopped working. However, at least it would reduce the financial pain of surviving on one income and offer a choice for parents who would prefer to stay at home but cannot afford to do so. Another positive step would be to promote more active pastimes through public education programmes.

To conclude, while it is improbable that any solution will be found in the near future, I feel that the abovementioned measures would be a good first step.

(280 words)

Model Answer B: IELTS Band 7$^+$

Divorce and family breakdown were virtually unheard of just 100 years ago. Now, however, almost half of all marriages fail. This phenomenon is symptomatic of the growing distance between family members in modern society. In this essay, I intend to explore the sources of this problem along with some possible solutions to it.

Chief among the causes of this problem is the modern lifestyle. Today's parents have to work harder than those of previous generations to support their families. Traditionally, one parent assumed the role of breadwinner, while the other—typically the mother—acted as the homemaker. Recently, though, double income families have become the norm. Consequently, an increasing number of children now grow up in a parentless environment. Little wonder, then, that they feel alienated. Another contributing factor is the passive and solitary nature of many modern forms of entertainment.

In order to resolve this sense of alienation within families, I believe we must first address its root causes. Perhaps the most effective method of doing this would be for governments to offer financial incentives to parents who choose to remain at home and take care of their families. Admittedly, such incentives would probably not fully compensate couples for lost income; however, they would at least soften the hardship of living on a single income and provide an alternative for parents who would rather remain at home but are unable to do so because of financial constraints. One further measure would be to promote more interactive leisure activities in the community through public education campaigns.

In conclusion, I believe that this is clearly a problem of such complexity that no solution is likely in the short term. However, I believe that the measures outlined above would constitute a good first step.

(292 words)

Model Sentence Structures 句型示范

Sentence 1	IELTS 5	Divorce and family breakdown were very unusual in the past.
	IELTS 6	Divorce and family breakdown were almost unheard of in the past.
	IELTS 7+	Divorce and family breakdown were virtually unheard of just 100 years ago.
Sentence 2	IELTS 5	The modern way of life is the main cause of this problem.
	IELTS 6	The chief cause of this problem is the modern way of life.
	IELTS 7+	Chief among the causes of this problem is the modern lifestyle.
Sentence 3	IELTS 5	However, double income families have become more common recently.
	IELTS 6	Recently, however, double income families have become more normal.
	IELTS 7+	Recently, though, double income families have become the norm.
Sentence 4	IELTS 5	So more and more children now grow up without their parents at home.
	IELTS 6	As a result, more and more children now grow up in a parentless environment.
	IELTS 7+	Consequently, an increasing number of children now grow up in a parentless environment.

Sentence 5	IELTS 5	So it is not surprising that they do not feel close (to their families).
	IELTS 6	It is no wonder, then, that they do not feel close (to their families).
	IELTS 7^+	Little wonder, then, that they feel alienated (from their families).
Sentence 6	IELTS 5	One other cause of this problem is modern entertainment.
	IELTS 6	Another factor that adds to this problem is that many types of modern entertainment are passive and designed for one person.
	IELTS 7^+	Another contributing factor is the passive and solitary nature of many modern forms of entertainment.

Academic Vocabulary 高分词汇

Basic 基础 5分	Intermediate 中级 6分	Advanced 高级 7分
	discuss (v.)	explore (v.)
	cause (n./v.)	source (n.) contributing factor
	recently (adv.)	in recent times
		offer (n./v.) provide (v.)
		chief (n./adj.) primary (adj.)
	traditionally (adv.) in the past	
usually (adv.)		typically (adv.)
		consequently (adv.) as a result
more and more		an increasing number of
		little wonder/ it is unsurprising
	resolve (v.)	address (v.) overcome (v.)
	feel (v.) believe (v.)	
		subsidy (n.) financial incentive
	of course	admittedly (adv.)
choice (n.)		alternative (n.)
look after/ take care of		
	programme (n.)	campaign (n./v.)

Basic 基础 5+分	Intermediate 中级 6+分	Advanced 高级 7+分
	would prefer to	would rather
stay (v.)		remain (v.)
cannot (do)		(be) unable to (do)
	leisure activity	pastime (n.)
	another (adj.) one other	one further
	to conclude/ in conclusion	
step (n.)		measure (n.)
		abovementioned (adj.) outlined above

Test Your Comprehension 综合练习

Answer these questions by circling A, B or C

1. Question 19 asks you to:
   A. say why families are not so close and what can be done to improve the situation
   B. say what the effects of family problems are and offer some solutions to the problem
   C. discuss whether or not families are as close as they used to be

2. Which of the following is the best sentence to use in academic writing?
   A. Now, however, almost half of all marriages fail.
   B. However, now almost half of all marriages fail.
   C. But now nearly half of all marriages fail.

3. The introduction to Model Answer B says that:
   A. divorce was very unusual 100 years ago
   B. many people have gotten divorced in the past 100 years
   C. divorce was illegal 100 years ago

4. The second paragraph of both model answers is about:
   A. problems with the modern lifestyle
   B. watching television
   C. both parents working

Answer these questions by writing YES or NO

5. Question 19 asks you to talk about families who live far away from each other.

6. The writer gives three examples of the modern lifestyle in both model answers.

7. "***Is symptomatic of***" (see Model Answer B) means "***is a sign of***".

8. "***Of course***" (see Model Answer A) and "***admittedly***" (see Model Answer B) are opposites.

9. The writer suggests that governments should give money to parents who stay at home to raise their children (see both model answers).

10. The writer suggests that mothers should stay at home instead of working (see Model Answer B).

11. Model Answer B concludes by saying that this problem will probably be solved soon.

Check your answers

1. **A**

The question says "***discuss the causes of this problem and offer some possible solutions to it***".

2. **A**

"***However***" is better than "***but***" in academic writing, and it is often better to place "***however***" after the adverb of time or after the subject of the sentence.

3. **A**

The phrase "***virtually unheard of***" means "***very unusual***".

4. **A**

"***Problems with the modern lifestyle***" is the topic of the paragraph. "***Watching television***" and "***both parents working***" are examples of this.

5. **NO**

The question asks you to talk about families who feel far away from each other.

6. **NO**

The writer only gives two examples—both parents working and modern entertainment.

7. **YES**

The word "***symptomatic***" sounds good in academic writing.

8. **NO**

These words mean the same thing in the context of this essay (they are synonyms).

9. **YES**

The writer says that governments should subsidise or give financial incentives to parents who stay at home to raise their children.

10. **NO**

The writer says that a parent should stay at home, but does not say that it must be the mother.

11. **NO**

It says we probably will not solve this problem anytime soon.

Question 20 Declining Educational Standards 教育水准下滑

WRITING TASK 2

You should spend about 40 minutes on this task.

Write about the following topic:

> ***Many people believe that educational standards have declined in recent times, particularly in the areas of literacy and numeracy.***
>
> ***Discuss the causes of this problem and offer some possible solutions to it.***

Write at least 250 words.

Model Answer A: IELTS Band 5^+

The issue of falling educational standards is of great importance in the world today. In this essay, I will briefly discuss some of the main causes of this problem and also offer some possible solutions to it.

In my view, one of the main reasons for poor quality education is that school students are not disciplined properly. In the past, teachers could smack or cane children who misbehaved. Now, however, this kind of punishment is not allowed and many teachers are losing control of their students as a result. If students do not listen, teachers cannot teach and learning becomes impossible. Clearly, discipline must be restored if we are to improve educational standards. Of course, there are many other ways to discipline children; however, I would argue that physical punishment is still the most effective method.

Another reason for poor reading, writing and mathematical skills among students today is that many schools waste too much time teaching "soft" subjects like music, art and drama. These subjects are certainly interesting. However, they tend to distract students from more important subjects like mathematics and English. The more time a student spends learning how to paint, the less time they spend learning how to read. Thus, in order to improve basic literacy and numeracy, I would argue that schools should focus their attention on core subjects.

In conclusion, this is such a complex problem that I don't believe any real solution will be found in the near future. However, I am convinced that the steps mentioned above would be helpful.

(258 words)

Model Answer B: IELTS Band 7^+

There is a widely held perception in many parts of the world today that educational standards are in decline. In the following essay, I aim to identify the sources of this problem as well as some viable solutions to it.

From my perspective, one of the most significant obstacles to learning in schools today is lack of discipline. While the teachers of previous generations were able to maintain order through the use of corporal punishment, such methods are no longer permitted. This has left many teachers powerless to control unruly students. The resultant misbehaviour and inattention on the part of students seriously undermines the learning process. If education standards are to be raised, therefore, it is crucial that classroom discipline be restored. Admittedly, there are numerous alternatives to corporal punishment, which is frowned upon by many these days. Nonetheless, I remain firmly convinced that physical forms of punishment are often the most effective method of behaviour management.

Another major contributing factor in the sub-standard academic achievement of today's students is the undue attention that many schools give to "soft" subjects like music, art and drama. Interesting though they may be, these subjects simply serve to distract students from more important and practical subjects like mathematics and English. The more time a student spends learning how to paint, for instance, the less time they spend learning how to read. In order to improve educational outcomes, therefore, we must ensure that core subjects are not neglected.

In reality, of course, this is a vast oversimplification of the issue. Solutions such as the reintroduction of corporal punishment would be problematic in themselves. However, I believe that the hard way is sometimes the best way.

(281 words)

Model Sentence Structures 句型示范

Sentence 1	IELTS 5	The falling quality of education is a very important matter in the world today.
	IELTS 6	The falling standard of education is an issue of great importance in the world today.
	IELTS 7+	The issue of falling educational standards is of great importance in the world today.
Sentence 2	IELTS 6	If students spend more time learning to paint, they spend less time learning to read.
	IELTS 7+	The more time a student spends learning how to paint, the less time they spend learning how to read.
Sentence 3	IELTS 5	Many people in the world today believe that the quality of education is falling.
	IELTS 6	Many people in the world today hold the perception that educational standards are declining.
	IELTS 7+	There is a widely held perception in many parts of the world today that educational standards are in decline.
Sentence 4	IELTS 5	In my opinion, what prevents students from learning in schools today is that they are not disciplined.
	IELTS 6	From my perspective, one of the greatest barriers to learning in schools today is that students lack discipline.
	IELTS 7+	From my perspective, one of the most significant obstacles to learning in schools today is lack of discipline.

Sentence 5	IELTS 5	These subjects are interesting. However, they just prevent students from concentrating on more important and practical subjects like mathematics and English.
	IELTS 6	Although these subjects are interesting, they simply distract students from more important and practical subjects like mathematics and English.
	IELTS 7^+	Interesting though they may be, these subjects simply serve to distract students from more important and practical subjects like mathematics and English.
Sentence 6	IELTS 5	Of course, the truth is that this question is not really so simple.
	IELTS 6	In truth, of course, this is an oversimplification of the matter.
	IELTS 7^+	In reality, of course, this is a vast oversimplification of the issue.

Academic Vocabulary 高分词汇

Basic 基础 5+分	Intermediate 中级 6分	Advanced 高级 7分
	fall (n./v.)	decline (n./v.)
	poor quality	sub-standard (adj.)
smack or cane	discipline (n./v.) punish (v.)	
	physical punishment	corporal punishment
	cause (n./v.) reason (n.)	factor (n.) source (n.)
important (adj.)		crucial (adj.)
	in my view	from my perspective
	allow (v.)	permit (v.)
		major (adj.) significant (adj.)
important subject		core subject
	therefore (adv.)	thus (adv.)
	however (adv.)	nonetheless (adv.)
like (prep.)	such as	
	of course	admittedly (adv.)

Test Your Comprehension 综合练习

Answer these questions by circling A, B or C

Questions 1-3 refer to the following four simplified sentences based on the above essays.

> i. **Now, however, this kind of punishment is not allowed.**
> ii. **In the past, teachers could smack naughty children.**
> iii. **Thus, students are becoming more and more difficult to control and this makes teaching impossible.**
> iv. **Educational standards are falling because school students are not disciplined properly.**

1. Put the above sentences in the correct order.
   A. ii. / i / iii. / iv.
   B. iv. / ii. / i. / iii.
   C. ii. / i. / iv. / iii.

2. Which of the above sentences is the most general?
   A. i.
   B. ii.
   C. iii.
   D. iv.

3. Which of the above sentences focuses on the effects of poor discipline?
   A. i.
   B. ii.
   C. iii.
   D. iv.

4. Which of these two simplified introductions is better?
   A. Many people believe that educational standards are falling. In this essay, I will discuss the causes of this problem and also some ways to resolve it.
   B. In this essay, I will discuss the causes of falling educational standards and also some ways to resolve this problem. Many people believe that educational standards are in decline.

5. An "***obstacle***" (see Model Answer B) is something that:
   A. stops you
   B. helps you
   C. teaches you

Answer these questions by writing YES or NO

6. The question asks you whether or not educational standards have fallen.

7. The writer mentions causes and solutions in different paragraphs (see both model answers).

8. The writer says that physical punishment is cruel and unnecessary (see both model answers).

9. "***Thus***" (see Model Answer A) and "***therefore***" (see Model Answer B) mean the same thing.

10. In the conclusion of Model Answer B, the writer discusses some weaknesses in the solutions he has suggested.

Check your answers

1. **B**

   The writer starts with a very general sentence, then talks about the past, the present and the final result. This is a logical way to write a paragraph and makes it easier to read.

2. **D**

3. **C**

   The word "***thus***" is a clue. It is often used when talking about results or effects.

4. **A**

   It is more logical to say what you will talk about at the end of your introduction, not the beginning.

5. **A**

   An "***obstacle***" is a "***barrier***".

6. **NO**

   It asks you why educational standards have fallen and how we can resolve this problem.

7. **NO**

   Paragraphs 2 and 3 contain one cause and one solution each.

8. **NO**

   The writer says that physical punishment is both important and necessary.

9. **YES**

   These words are synonyms.

10. **YES**

    If you have to make some suggestions, it may be possible to discuss remaining questions or possible challenges in the implementation of your solutions towards the end of your essay. However, you must be careful not to undermine your arguments.

IELTS

WRITE RIGHT

培训类写作 TASK 1

Writing Task 1: General Training Module

Question Types

In General Training Writing Task 1 you will be asked to write a letter of at least 150 words. Although General Training Writing Task 1 is somewhat easier than Academic Writing Task 1, it is still a challenge for most candidates and there are still several different question types that you must prepare for.

Firstly, you should practise writing letters to people you know and also to people who you do not know. Letters to people you know should have an informal, friendly style, whereas letters to people you do not know should be more formal. Therefore, this section highlights some of the differences between informal and formal English.

You should also practise writing letters with different purposes. You must be able to write letters of request, complaint, enquiry, apology, explanation and thanks. Do not forget that many letters have several purposes: for example, you may wish to complain about poor service you received at a hotel and request an apology or explanation.

The following are examples of the two main question types you are likely to face, taken from the model questions below.

1. Formal Letter

正式信件

WRITING TASK 1

You should spend about 20 minutes on this task.

You recently went to Australia for a holiday. However, your return flight was delayed by a day.

Write a letter to the airline company. In your letter

- ***Introduce yourself***
- ***Complain about the delay***
- ***Explain the problems that it caused you***
- ***Ask for a letter of apology and/or some form of compensation***

Write at least 150 words.

You do **NOT** need to write any addresses.

Begin your letter as follows:

Dear ...,

2. Informal Letter

非正式信件

WRITING TASK 1

You should spend about 20 minutes on this task.

An old friend of yours is coming to visit your city. You had planned to meet him at the airport, but something has come up and you will not be able to make it there on time.

Write to your friend. In your letter

- ***Explain the situation***
- ***Offer to make alternate arrangements***

Write at least 150 words.

You do **NOT** need to write any addresses.

Begin your letter as follows:

Dear ...,

Formal Letter
正式信件

Question 21 Internet Connection Problems
网络问题

WRITING TASK 1

You should spend about 20 minutes on this task.

> ***You are a university student living in on-campus accommodation. You are having some problems with the internet connection in your room.***
>
> ***Write to the supervisor of your residence. In your letter***
>
> - ***Introduce yourself***
> - ***Inform him/her of the situation***
> - ***Request that the problem be fixed***

Write at least 150 words.

You do **NOT** need to write any addresses.

Begin your letter as follows:

Dear ...,

Model Answer A: IELTS Band 5^+

Dear Harold,

I'm Jenny Chen—a new overseas student now staying in Unit 5 of Cassowary House. So far I've found it pretty comfortable here, but I'm not totally satisfied with the university's internet system. Your student accommodation brochure said that I would have full internet access in my room, but when I tried to use MSN Messenger and other communication programs they didn't work properly. I talked to some of my housemates about the problem and they told me that the university has actually blocked these programs. I'm sure you realise that international phone calls are very expensive compared to chatting online. I think it's really unfair to stop overseas students like me from finding cheaper ways to keep in touch with our friends and family at home, especially since we pay such high tuition fees. Could you please unblock these programs so that we can use them? Thanks very much for your help.

Regards,
Jenny Chen

(158 words)

Model Answer B: IELTS Band 7^+

Dear Mr Jones,

My name is Jenny Chen—a recently arrived overseas student currently staying in Unit 5 of Cassowary House. While I have found most of the facilities here quite satisfactory thus far, I wish to lodge a complaint about the university's internet system. Your student accommodation brochure, which I read closely prior to booking this room, indicated that I would have unlimited access to the Internet. Upon arrival, however, I discovered that MSN Messenger and other such internet communication programs would not run properly. I discussed the matter with some of my fellow students who informed me that these programs had been blocked by the university. As you are no doubt aware, international phone calls are incredibly expensive by comparison with chatting online. Considering the high tuition fees we overseas students already pay, I feel it is entirely unreasonable to prevent us from seeking more affordable alternatives when it comes to communicating with loved ones at home. I was, therefore, wondering if you could unblock these programs? Your assistance in this matter is greatly appreciated.

Yours sincerely,
Jenny Chen

(181 words)

Model Sentence Structures 句型示范

Sentence 1	IELTS 5	I think most of the facilities here are pretty good, but I want to complain about the university's internet system.
	IELTS 6	So far I have found most of the facilities here quite satisfactory. However, I wish to complain about the university's internet system.
	IELTS 7+	While I have found most of the facilities here quite satisfactory thus far, I wish to lodge a complaint about the university's internet system.
Sentence 2	IELTS 5	I read your student accommodation brochure before I booked this room. It said that I would have full internet access.
	IELTS 6	I read your student accommodation brochure prior to booking this room and it indicated that I would have unlimited access to the Internet.
	IELTS 7+	Your student accommodation brochure, which I read closely prior to booking this room, indicated that I would have unlimited access to the Internet.
Sentence 3	IELTS 5	But when I arrived, I found out that MSN Messenger and other internet communication programs did not work properly.
	IELTS 6	However, upon arrival I found that MSN Messenger and other similar internet communication programs would not work properly.
	IELTS 7+	Upon arrival, however, I discovered that MSN Messenger and other such internet communication programs would not run properly.

Sentence 4	IELTS 5	So could you please unblock these programs?
	IELTS 6	Therefore, I was wondering if you could unblock these programs?
	IELTS 7^+	I was, therefore, wondering if you could unblock these programs?
Sentence 5	IELTS 5	Thanks very much for your help.
	IELTS 6	I really appreciate your assistance in this matter.
	IELTS 7^+	Your assistance in this matter is greatly appreciated.

Academic Vocabulary 高分词汇

Basic 基础 informal	Intermediate 中级	Advanced 高级 formal
new (adj.)		recently arrived
so far		thus far
pretty (adv.)	quite (adv.)	
say (v.)		indicate (v.)
work properly	run properly	
problem (n.)		matter (n.)
tell (v.)		inform (v.)
	realise (v.)	(be) aware
very (adv.)		incredibly (adv.)
compared to		by comparison with
unfair (adj.)		unreasonable (adj.)
stop (v.)		prevent (v.)
cheaper (adj.)		more affordable
keep in touch	communicate (v.)	
help (n./v.)		assistance (n.)

Test Your Comprehension 综合练习

Answer these questions by circling A, B or C

1. Question 21 asks you to write a letter to:
   A. someone you know well
   B. someone you may have met but do not know well
   C. someone you have never met

2. This letter should be:
   A. friendly
   B. informal
   C. formal

3. The purpose of this letter is to:
   A. make an enquiry
   B. make a complaint
   C. make a complaint and a request

4. How does the writer start these two letters?
   A. She introduces herself.
   B. She says why she is writing.
   C. She gives her contact details.

5. Which of the following is the most formal?
   A. make a complaint
   B. lodge a complaint
   C. complain

Answer these questions by writing YES or NO

6. It is acceptable to use contractions like "***I'm***" and "***didn't***" in formal letters.

7. The writer makes up extra details about the situation that are not included in the question.

8. The writer asks the supervisor of the residence to help her and then explains the situation.

9. "***Considering***" (see Model Answer B) means "***because of***".

10. "***Yours sincerely***" (see Model Answer B) is a good way to finish a letter if you do not know a person's name and have never met him/her before.

Check your answers

1. **B**

   You have probably met the supervisor of your residence before, but the question does not make this clear.

2. **C**

   The letter should be formal because you do not know the person well. Therefore, Model Answer B is better.

3. **C**

   You do not just want to complain. You also want the supervisor to do something about the situation.

4. **A**

   It is usually a good idea to introduce yourself if you do not know the recipient well.

5. **B**

6. **NO**

   Contractions should not be used in formal writing.

7. **YES**

   It is very difficult to write this kind of letter without including detail. Use your imagination and make up a story.

8. **NO**

   The writer explains the situation and then makes a request.

9. **YES**

   "***Considering***" is better because it is more formal.

10. **NO**

    "***Yours sincerely***" is usually used to sign off on a letter to someone whose name you know but you have never met.

Question 22 Delayed Flight 班机延误

WRITING TASK 1

You should spend about 20 minutes on this task.

You recently went to Australia for a holiday. However, your return flight was delayed by a day.

Write a letter to the airline company. In your letter

- ***Introduce yourself***
- ***Complain about the delay***
- ***Explain the problems that it caused you***
- ***Ask for a letter of apology and/or some form of compensation***

Write at least 150 words.

You do **NOT** need to write any addresses.

Begin your letter as follows:

Dear ...,

Model Answer A: IELTS Band 5^+

To Customer Service,

I am writing to you about a last-minute delay in a flight I took with your airline last week. I was supposed to fly to Sydney from Beijing on December 14 and come back on January 28. The first part of the trip was fine, but there was a problem on the way home. After I checked in, spent all the Australian dollars I had left in the airport duty-free shops and went to the boarding lounge, I was told I would have to spend a night in Brunei on the way home. This was really inconvenient for me and also for my company because I was scheduled to start work the next day. Since your airline was to blame for this problem, I think you really should give me something to make up for it. Actually, I think it would be fair if you gave me a free return ticket to Australia. I've written my contact details at the top of the page. By the way, could you please deal with this quickly? Thanks.

Regards,
Tony Yu

(182 words)

Model Answer B: IELTS Band 7+

Dear Sir/Madam,

I am writing with regard to an unexpected delay in a flight I took with your airline recently. I was initially booked to leave Beijing for Sydney on the 14th of December and return on the 28th of January. The first leg of the journey was uneventful enough. However, on arrival in the boarding lounge at Kingsford Smith Airport, I was informed that my return flight would be delayed by 14 hours and that I would have to spend one night in Brunei on my way back to Taiwan. This caused considerable inconvenience, not only to myself but also to my employers, as I was due to commence work again the following day. In fact, it almost cost me my job. Given the fact that this foul-up occurred at such short notice and was entirely the fault of your airline, I feel that compensation in the form of a complimentary ticket of the same distance would be warranted. I can be contacted at the address supplied. A swift response would be greatly appreciated.

Yours faithfully,
Tony Yu

(179 words)

Model Sentence Structures 句型示范

Sentence 1	IELTS 5	I am writing to you about a last-minute delay in a flight I took with your airline last week.
	IELTS 6	I am writing to you regarding an unexpected delay in a flight I took with your airline recently.
	IELTS 7+	I am writing with regard to an unexpected delay in a flight I took with your airline recently.
Sentence 2	IELTS 5	Originally, I booked a flight from Beijing to Sydney on December 14 and from Sydney to Beijing on January 28.
	IELTS 6	Initially, I was booked to leave Beijing for Sydney on December 14 and come back on January 28.
	IELTS 7+	I was initially booked to leave Beijing for Sydney on the 14th of December and return on the 28th of January.
Sentence 3	IELTS 5	Because this problem happened so suddenly and your airline was completely to blame, I think you should give me something to make up for it.
	IELTS 6	Given the suddenness of the delay and the fact that your airline was entirely to blame for this foul-up, I feel that you should compensate me by giving me a free ticket of the same distance.
	IELTS 7+	Given the fact that this foul-up occurred at such short notice and was entirely the fault of your airline, I feel that compensation in the form of a complimentary ticket of the same distance would be warranted.

Sentence 4	IELTS 6	You can contact me at the address I have given.
	IELTS 7^+	I can be contacted at the address supplied.
Sentence 5	IELTS 6	I would greatly appreciate a quick reply.
	IELTS 7^+	A swift response would be greatly appreciated.

Academic Vocabulary 高分词汇

Basic 基础 informal	Intermediate 中级	Advanced 高级 formal
about (prep.)		with regard to
come back	return (v.)	
part of the trip		leg of the journey
	trip (n.)	journey (n.)
but (adv./conj.)	however (adv.)	
tell (v.)		inform (v.)
company (n.)		employers (n.)
start (n./v.)		commence (v.)
because (conj.)		since (conj.) given the fact that
problem (n.)		foul-up
free (adj.)		complimentary (adj.)

Test Your Comprehension 综合练习

Answer these questions by circling A, B or C

1. Question 22 asks you to write to:
   A. an acquaintance
   B. a stranger
   C. a friend

2. This letter should be:
   A. informal
   B. semi-formal
   C. formal

3. Which of the following is the best way to start a formal letter to someone if you do not know their name?
   A. To Customer Service
   B. To Whom it May Concern
   C. Dear Sir/Madam

4. Which of the following should not be used in formal writing?
   A. I feel
   B. I believe
   C. I think

5. Which of the following phrases is best in formal writing?
   A. I am writing to you about...
   B. I am writing with regard to...
   C. I am writing this letter because I want to...

Answer these questions by writing YES or NO

6. The question tells me what my flight dates were and where I travelled to.

7. The writer mentions the consequences of the flight delay before making his request.

8. "***By the way***" (see Model Answer A) is informal and should only be used in speaking.

9. "***Yours faithfully***" is used to sign off when you know a person's name, but have never met him/her before.

Check your answers

1. **B**
   This is not mentioned in the question, but it is unlikely that you have met the person you are writing to. In any case, you certainly do not know him/her well.

2. **C**
   This is a serious letter to someone you do not know well.

3. **C**
   This is the normal way to start a formal letter if you do not know the recipient's name.

4. **C**
   "***I think***" is often used in speaking.

5. **B**

6. **NO**
   The writer made these details up. Be creative—try making up extra detail to make your letter sound more natural.

7. **YES**
   The writer explains the problem and its consequences and then asks for compensation.

8. **YES**
   "***By the way***" is for speaking and informal writing. It is not for formal writing.

9. **NO**
   "***Yours faithfully***" is a good way to sign off if you do not know the other person's name.

Question 23 Problems with a Rented Car
租车问题

WRITING TASK 1

You should spend about 20 minutes on this task.

You rented a car recently, but were not satisfied with it.

Write a letter of complaint to the rental agency. In your letter

- ***Introduce yourself***
- ***Explain what went wrong with the car you rented***
- ***Ask for some form of compensation***

Write at least 150 words.

You do **NOT** need to write any addresses.

Begin your letter as follows:

Dear ...,

Model Answer A: IELTS Band 5^+

Dear Sir,

I'm writing because I was not very happy with a car I hired from your company a few weeks ago. When I picked it up from your city office, I saw that there was lots of smoke coming from the back. I told your employee, Rick, that I needed a reliable car because I was going to drive it a long way. He promised me that the car was fine and said I wouldn't have any problems with it. But when I drove it in the country it broke down and I got stuck 200 kilometres from the nearest town. And do you know what happened next? The air conditioner broke. It was terrible. After I waited for help and then waited for the car to be fixed, I had to drive it without an air conditioner in the middle of summer. I rented that car because of what your employee said, so I think you should give me my money back. Anyway, I've written my phone number and address at the top of the page. Could you deal with this quickly please? Thank you.

Regards,
Jamie Wang

(190 words)

Model Answer B: IELTS Band 7+

Dear Sir/Madam,

I am writing this letter in order to complain about a car that I rented from your agency recently. When I collected it from your city branch, I noticed clouds of smoke coming from the exhaust pipe. I told your representative that I required a dependable vehicle as I would be making a long journey, and he assured me that I would not have any mechanical difficulties with it. However, as soon as I took it for a longer trip it broke down, leaving me stranded 200 kilometres from the nearest town. To make matters worse, the air-conditioning stopped working as well. Consequently, after several hours of waiting, first for help and then for repairs, I had to drive on in the summer heat. Since I rented this car on your representative's advice, I feel that I am entitled to request a full refund. I can be contacted at the address or phone number provided. I would greatly appreciate your prompt resolution of this matter.

Yours faithfully,
Jamie Wang

(171 words)

Model Sentence Structures 句型示范

Sentence 1	IELTS 5	I am writing because I want to complain about a car I rented from your company a few weeks ago.
	IELTS 6	I am writing this letter to complain about a car I rented from your agency recently.
	IELTS 7^+	I am writing this letter in order to complain about a car that I rented from your company recently.
Sentence 2	IELTS 6	When I picked it up from your city office, I saw that there was smoke coming from the exhaust pipe.
	IELTS 7^+	When I collected it from your city branch, I noticed clouds of smoke coming from the exhaust pipe.
Sentence 3	IELTS 5	I told your employee I needed a car that would not break down because I wanted to drive it a long way, and he promised me that I would not have any problems with it.
	IELTS 6	I told your representative that I required a reliable car as I would be driving it a long way, and he assured me that I would not have any mechanical problems with it.
	IELTS 7^+	I told your representative that I required a dependable vehicle as I would be making a long journey, and he assured me that I would not have any mechanical difficulties with it.

Sentence 4	**IELTS 5**	So after I spent several hours waiting for help and repairs, I had to keep driving in really hot weather.
	IELTS 6	Consequently, after I spent several hours waiting, first for help and then for repairs, I had to continue driving in the hot sun.
	IELTS 7+	Consequently, after several hours of waiting, first for help and then for repairs, I had to drive on in the summer heat.
Sentence 5	**IELTS 5**	Because your employee convinced me to rent this car, I think you should give me my money back.
	IELTS 6	Since your representative convinced me to rent this car, I feel it is my right to ask for a full refund.
	IELTS 7+	Since I rented this car on your representative's advice, I feel that I am entitled to request a full refund.
Sentence 6	**IELTS 5**	Could you please deal with this matter quickly?
	IELTS 6	I would appreciate it if you could resolve this matter promptly.
	IELTS 7+	I would greatly appreciate your prompt resolution of this matter.

Academic Vocabulary 高分词汇

Basic 基础 informal	Intermediate 中级	Advanced 高级 formal
	hire (v.) rent (v.)	
company (n.)	agency (n.)	
a few weeks ago	recently (adv.)	
pick up	collect (v.)	
city office	city branch	
see (v.)	notice (v.)	
	employee (n.)	representative (n.)
	promise (n./v.)	assure (v.)
		dependable (adj.) reliable (adj.)
car (n.)		vehicle (n.)
	trip (n.)	journey (n.)
	stuck (adj.)	stranded (adj.)
but (adv./conj.)	however (adv.)	
so (adv./conj.)		consequently (adv.)
because (conj.)		since (conj.)
deal with		resolve (v.)
quick (adj.)		prompt (adj.)

Test Your Comprehension 综合练习

Answer these questions by circling A, B or C

1. Question 23 asks you to write:
   A. a formal letter to someone you know
   B. an informal letter to someone you do not know
   C. a formal letter to someone you do not know well

Questions 2-3 refer to the following four simplified sentences taken from the model answers.

> i. **However, when I took it for a longer trip it broke down.**
> ii. **Your employee told me that the car I rented would not have any problems.**
> iii. **I wish to complain about a car that I rented from your agency recently.**
> iv. **Therefore, I feel that you should give me my money back.**

2. Put the above sentences in the correct order.
   A. i. / ii. / iii. / iv.
   B. iv. / ii. / iii. / i.
   C. iii. / ii. / i. / iv.

3. Which of these sentences says why the writer wrote the letter?
   A. i.
   B. ii.
   C. iii.
   D. iv.

4. In Model Answer B, the word "*since*" means:
   A. after
   B. because
   C. when

Answer these questions by writing YES or NO

5. "***Dear Sir***" (see Model Answer A) is a good way to start any formal letter if you do not know the person you are writing to.

6. Past tense is used in this letter.

7. "***And***" is a good way to start a sentence (see Model Answer A).

8. "***And do you know what happened next?***" (see Model Answer A) is too informal for this letter and sounds silly.

9. "***Had to***" (see both model answers) is the past tense of "***have to***".

10. "***Resolution***" is the noun for "***resolve***" (see Model Answer B).

Check your answers

1. **C**

It asks you to write to the rental agency, so the letter is formal. Model Answer B is better.

2. **C**

The writer explains why he is writing, gives background information and then makes a request. This is a logical way to organise this kind of letter.

3. **C**

4. **B**

"***Since***" sometimes means "***after***", but in this case it means "***because***".

5. **NO**

This is not correct because the recipient may be a woman.

6. **YES**

Past tense is used to explain what happened.

7. **NO**

You should not start sentences with "***and***" in formal, written English. Use "***in addition***" or "***additionally***" instead.

8. **YES**

Do not directly ask the recipient questions. It sounds silly.

9. **YES**

10. **YES**

Question 24 Low IELTS Score
IELTS成绩不佳

WRITING TASK 1

You should spend about 20 minutes on this task.

You have just received a letter from an overseas university saying that your IELTS band score of 6 is too low for admission to any of its Master's courses (You need 6.5).

Write a letter to the admissions officer. In your letter

- ***Introduce yourself***
- ***Enquire about any alternative ways of gaining entrance***

Write at least 150 words.

You do **NOT** need to write any addresses.

Begin your letter as follows:

Dear ...,

Model Answer A: IELTS Band 5^+

Dear Wendy,

Hi. I just got a letter from you saying that I can't enter your university's Master of Marketing Management course in August because my English isn't good enough. You said my IELTS score of 6 was too low and that I would need at least 6.5. I know it's important for overseas candidates to have good English, but I really want to go to your university. Is there any way I could convince you to change your mind? Also, a friend of mine who is now studying at your university told me I might be able to do a two-month, pre-sessional course and then sit a different test (or take IELTS again) before the start of semester because that's what she did. So I wanted to ask for more information about any courses like this or any other way to get in to your Marketing programme. I've written my home and e-mail addresses as well as my phone number at the bottom of the page if you need them. Thank you for your help.

Regards,
Yung, Da Wei

(180 words)

Model Answer B: IELTS Band 7⁺

Dear Ms Barlowe,

I am writing with regard to your rejection of my application to begin postgraduate studies in Marketing Management at your university in August. You indicated that my IELTS band score of 6 was insufficient and that I would require a minimum of 6.5 to gain admission. While I recognise the importance of ensuring the English competency of enrolling overseas candidates and fully accept your decision, a friend of mine currently studying at your institution has suggested that it may be possible for me to take a two-month, pre-sessional English course and then either take an internal examination or resit IELTS prior to the beginning of semester as this is what she did. Hence, I was wondering if you could send me further information on any such courses on offer or any other possible means of gaining entrance to your Master of Marketing Management programme. I have supplied my home and e-mail addresses along with my mobile phone number for your convenience. Your assistance in this matter is greatly appreciated.

Yours sincerely,
Yung, Da Wei

(177 words)

Model Sentence Structures 句型示范

Sentence 1	IELTS 5	I am writing about your letter saying that I will not be able to enter your university's Master of Marketing Management course in August.
	IELTS 6	I am writing with regard to your letter rejecting my application to start postgraduate studies in Marketing Management at your university in August.
	IELTS 7+	I am writing with regard to your rejection of my application to begin postgraduate studies in Marketing Management at your university in August.
Sentence 2	IELTS 6	You said that my IELTS score of 6 was too low and that I would need at least 6.5 to get in.
	IELTS 7+	You indicated that my IELTS band score of 6 was insufficient and that I would require a minimum of 6.5 to gain admission.
Sentence 3	IELTS 5	I know it is important to make sure new overseas candidates have good English and I fully accept your decision. However, a friend of mine who is now studying at your university has told me that I might be able to take a two-month, pre-sessional course and then do a different test or take IELTS again before the start of semester because that's what she did.
	IELTS 6	I recognise that it is important to ensure that new overseas candidates are competent in English and I fully accept your decision; however, a friend of mine who is currently studying at your institution has suggested that I may be able to take a two-month, pre-sessional English course and then take an internal test or sit IELTS again prior to the start of semester because this is what she did.

Sentence 3	IELTS 7+	While I recognise the importance of ensuring the English competency of enrolling overseas candidates and fully accept your decision, a friend of mine currently studying at your institution has suggested that it may be possible for me to take a two-month, pre-sessional English course and then either take an internal examination or resit IELTS prior to the beginning of semester as this is what she did.
Sentence 4	IELTS 5	So I wanted to ask for more information about any courses like this or any other way to get in to your Marketing programme.
	IELTS 6	Therefore, I wonder if you could send me more information on any courses like this or any other means of getting in to your Master of Marketing Management programme.
	IELTS 7+	Hence, I was wondering if you could send me information on any such courses on offer or any other possible means of gaining entrance to your Master of Marketing Management programme.
Sentence 5	IELTS 5	I have written my home and e-mail addresses as well as my phone number at the bottom of the page if you need them.
	IELTS 6	I have provided my home and e-mail addresses as well as my mobile phone number should you require them.
	IELTS 7+	I have supplied my home and e-mail addresses along with my mobile phone number for your convenience.
Sentence 6	IELTS 5	Thank you very much for your help.
	IELTS 6	I appreciate your assistance.
	IELTS 7+	Your assistance in this matter is greatly appreciated.

Academic Vocabulary 高分词汇

Basic 基础 informal	Intermediate 中级	Advanced 高级 formal
	course (n.)	*programme (n.)
say (v.)		indicate (v.)
score (n.)	band score	
get in	enter (v.)	gain entrance/ gain admission
too low	insufficient (adj.)	
need (n./v.)		require (v.)
	at least	a minimum of
know (v.)		recognise (v.)
now (adv.)		currently (adv.)
	university (n.)	institution (n.)
		take IELTS/ sit IELTS
test (n.)		examination (n.)
before (adv.)		prior to
because (conj.)		as (conj.)
so (adv./conj.)		hence (adv.)

Note: Americans write "program", whereas the British/Australian spelling of this word is "programme". We all write "program" when we talk about "computer programs".

Test Your Comprehension 综合练习

Answer these questions by circling A, B or C

1. Question 24 asks you to write:
   A. a formal letter
   B. an informal letter
   C. a normal letter

2. Which model answer is better?
   A. Model Answer A
   B. Model Answer B
   C. both equally good

3. "***Ms***" is a title for:
   A. a married woman
   B. an unmarried woman
   C. a married or unmarried woman

4. When the writer uses "***currently***" (see Model Answer B), what verb tense does he use?
   A. past simple tense (studied)
   B. present perfect tense (has/have studied)
   C. present continuous tense (is/are studying)

Answer these questions by writing YES or NO

5. The writer invented the recipient's name.

6. "***Hi***" (see Model Answer A) is too informal for this situation.

7. It is rude to directly ask someone to change their mind in this situation (see Model Answer A).

8. It is rude to ask if there is any other way to enter the course (see both model answers).

9. The phrase "***means of gaining entrance***" (see Model Answer B) is the same as "***way to get in***".

10. "***Yours sincerely***" is a good way to sign off if you know the other person's name but have never met them.

Check your answers

1. **A**

2. **B**

   Model Answer B is better because it is more formal.

3. **C**

   Many women like to use the title "***Ms***" nowadays because they feel that "***Miss***" and "***Mrs***" are sexist. "***Ms***" also sounds more professional.

4. **C**

   The word "***currently***" usually goes with present continuous tense; however, it can sometimes be used with present simple.

5. **YES**

6. **YES**

   You do not need to say hello in a formal letter.

7. **YES**

   It is pushy and rude to ask someone to change their mind, especially when an official decision has been made. In some cultures, it is acceptable to push someone to change their mind, but in English speaking countries it is not.

8. **NO**

   It is not rude to ask for information about other ways to get in to university.

9. **YES**

   These two phrases mean the same thing, but "***means of gaining entrance***" is better because it is more formal.

10. **YES**

    You should write this if you know the recipient's name but have never met him/her.

Question 25 University Clubs 学校社团

WRITING TASK 1

You should spend about 20 minutes on this task.

You have been accepted to study at an overseas university, but feel a little anxious about living and studying in an unfamiliar environment.

Write to the university's student union. In your letter

- ***Introduce yourself***
- ***Explain your interests***
- ***Enquire about any relevant social clubs you might be able to join***

Write at least 150 words.

You do **NOT** need to write any addresses.

Begin your letter as follows:

Dear ...,

Model Answer A: IELTS Band 5^+

To the Student Union,

Hello. I'm an overseas student taking up studies at your university soon. I wanted to ask about any clubs or societies that I might be able to join next semester. I'm a little bit worried about going to a university I don't know in a different country, so I want to make some contacts before I get there. I guess what I really want to know is whether or not there are any clubs for Chinese students. If there are, could you send me some information about their membership fees and how to join, or just give me their phone numbers so I can call them myself? I'm interested in computers and technology, online gaming and basketball so it would be great if you could send me information about any clubs for people who are interested in these things. Thanks very much for your help.

Best wishes,
Johnson Zhang

(153 words)

Model Answer B: IELTS Band 7⁺

Dear Sir/Madam,

I am a newly enrolled overseas student soon to take up studies at your university. I am writing with regard to any clubs or societies likely to be open and operating at your university during the coming semester. I am rather nervous about attending an unfamiliar university in a foreign country and would, therefore, like to make some contacts before arriving. I am especially interested to know whether there are any clubs for Chinese students. If so, could you possibly send me some brochures containing information on membership and associated fees, or at least provide me with the contact details of any such clubs so that I can make my own independent enquiries? I would also be grateful for any information you could provide about clubs related to computers and technology, online gaming or basketball, as these are areas of particular interest to me. Your assistance in this matter is greatly appreciated.

Yours faithfully,
Johnson Zhang

(158 words)

Model Sentence Structures 句型示范

Sentence 1	IELTS 5	I'm an overseas student starting studies at your university soon.
	IELTS 6	I am a newly enrolled overseas student taking up studies at your university soon.
	IELTS 7⁺	I am a newly enrolled overseas student soon to take up studies at your university.
Sentence 2	IELTS 5	I wanted to ask about any clubs or societies that I might be able to join next semester.
	IELTS 6	I am writing about any clubs or societies that may be open and running at your university next semester.
	IELTS 7⁺	I am writing with regard to any clubs or societies likely to be open and operating at your university during the coming semester.
Sentence 3	IELTS 5	I'm a little bit worried about going to a university I don't know in a different country, so I want to make some contacts before I get there.
	IELTS 6	I am quite nervous about attending a university I am unfamiliar with in a foreign country. Therefore, I would like to make some contacts before I arrive.
	IELTS 7⁺	I am rather nervous about attending an unfamiliar university in a foreign country and would, therefore, like to make some contacts before arriving.

Sentence 4	IELTS 5	What I really want to know is whether or not there are any clubs for Chinese students.
	IELTS 6	I am particularly interested to know if there are any clubs for Chinese students.
	IELTS 7+	I am especially interested to know whether there are any clubs for Chinese students.
Sentence 5	IELTS 5	If there are, could you send me some information about their membership fees and how to join, or just give me their phone numbers so I can call them myself.
	IELTS 6	If there are, could you possibly send me some brochures containing information about membership and associated fees, or just give me the phone numbers of any such clubs so that I can enquire independently.
	IELTS 7+	If so, could you possibly send me some brochures containing information on membership and associated fees, or at least provide me with the contact details of any such clubs so that I can make my own independent enquiries.
Sentence 6	IELTS 5	I'm interested in computers and technology, online gaming and basketball, so it would be great if you could send me information about any clubs for people who are interested in these things.
	IELTS 6	I would also appreciate any information you could give me about clubs related to computers and technology, online gaming or basketball, because I am particularly interested in these areas.
	IELTS 7+	I would also be grateful for any information you could provide about clubs related to computers and technology, online gaming or basketball, as these are areas of particular interest to me.

Academic Vocabulary 高分词汇

Basic 基础 informal	Intermediate 中级	Advanced 高级 formal
ask (v.)		enquire (v.)
	a little bit	rather (adv.)
worried (adj.)	nervous (adj.)	
go to		attend (v.)
different country	foreign country	
get there	arrive (v.)	
give (v.)		provide (v.)
	(be) grateful	appreciate (v.)
help (n./v.)		assistance (n.)

Test Your Comprehension 综合练习

Answer these questions by circling A, B or C

1. Question 25 asks you to write:
   A. a formal letter to someone you have probably met
   B. a formal letter to someone you have probably never met
   C. an informal letter to an old friend

2. The purpose of this letter is to:
   A. say how nervous you feel
   B. ask for information
   C. join a club

3. Which of the following is a better way to start a question in a formal letter?
   A. Tell me...
   B. I want to ask...
   C. I wanted to ask...

4. Which of the following is the best way to finish a formal letter to someone whose name you do not know?
   A. Best wishes
   B. Regards
   C. Yours faithfully

Answer these questions by writing YES or NO

5. The writer gives some information about himself before asking the recipient for information.

6. "***Hello***" (see Model Answer A) is a bad way to start a formal letter.

7. "***I guess***" (see Model Answer A) is too informal to use in this letter.

8. The writer puts "***therefore***" (see Model Answer B) at the start of the sentence.

9. Too many sentences in Model Answer B start with "***I am***".

Check your answers

1. **B**

2. **B**

   In this letter, you must ask for information about clubs and societies.

3. **C**

   Past tense is often considered more formal than present tense. For instance, "***could you tell me***" is more formal than "***can you tell me***".

4. **C**

   The other two alternatives are too informal.

5. **YES**

   This is polite.

6. **YES**

   You do not need to say "***hello***" or "***hi***" in a formal letter.

7. **YES**

   "***I guess***" is quite informal. Use it when speaking, but not in formal writing.

8. **NO**

   In Model Answer B, "***therefore***" comes in the middle of the two-word verb "***would like***", which becomes "***would, therefore, like***".

9. **YES**

   You should not start every sentence the same way. This is repetitive and boring and the examiner may think you do not know any other way to start a sentence.

Question 26 University Entrance Requirements 大学入学条件

WRITING TASK 1

You should spend about 20 minutes on this task.

You are thinking of applying to do postgraduate studies at an overseas university or college.

Write to the admissions office. In your letter

- ***Introduce yourself***
- ***Request information about entry requirements, tuition fees and the availability of accommodation on campus***

Write at least 150 words.

You do **NOT** need to write any addresses.

Begin your letter as follows:

Dear ...,

Model Answer A: IELTS Band 5⁺

To the Admissions Officer,

I just wanted to ask what academic, professional and English qualifications I would need to get into your MBA programme. At the moment, I've got a Bachelor of International Trade degree from a good Chinese university as well as three years' experience working in the field with a big company that sells computer parts. I haven't taken the IELTS test yet, but I got more than 600 in TOEFL last year. Is this good enough? I'd really appreciate any information you could give me about this. Also, could you send me some brochures about tuition fees and the availability and cost of student accommodation? I've sent copies of my academic transcript as well as work and academic references. If you need any more information about my background or study plans, you can get in touch with me at the address or phone number at the top of this page.

Regards,
Jack Peng

(157 words)

Model Answer B: IELTS Band 7^+

Dear Sir/Madam,

I am writing in order to enquire about the academic, professional and/or English language prerequisites for admission to your Master of Business Administration programme. I currently hold a Bachelor's degree in International Trade from a reputable Chinese university and have three years' relevant experience with a major distributor of computer components. I have not yet taken the IELTS test; however, I did attain a score of over 600 in TOEFL last year. I was wondering if this is likely to be sufficient? I would be most appreciative of any information you could give me in this regard. I also wonder if it would be possible for you to send brochures relating to tuition fees along with the availability and cost of on-campus accommodation. Please find enclosed copies of my academic transcript as well as both academic and work-related references. Should you have any further queries regarding my study plans or background, please do not hesitate to contact me at the address or phone number provided above.

Yours faithfully,
Jack Peng

(172 words)

Model Sentence Structures 句型示范

Sentence 1	IELTS 5	I wanted to ask about the study, work and/or English language requirements to enter your Master of Business Administration course.
	IELTS 6	I am writing to enquire about the academic, professional and/or English language requirements for entrance to your Master of Business Administration programme.
	IELTS 7+	I am writing in order to enquire about the academic, professional and/or English language prerequisites for admission to your Master of Business Administration programme.
Sentence 2	IELTS 5	Is this good enough?
	IELTS 6	I was wondering if this will be good enough?
	IELTS 7+	I was wondering if this is likely to be sufficient?
Sentence 3	IELTS 5	I would really appreciate any information you could give me about this.
	IELTS 6	I would most appreciate any information you could give me on this matter.
	IELTS 7+	I would be most appreciative of any information you could give me in this regard.

Sentence 4	IELTS 5	Could you please also send brochures about tuition fees as well as the availability and cost of accommodation at the university?
	IELTS 6	I also wonder if you could send brochures on tuition fees along with the availability and cost of accommodation on campus.
	IELTS 7+	I also wonder if it would be possible for you to send brochures relating to tuition fees along with the availability and cost of on-campus accommodation.
Sentence 5	IELTS 5	I have included copies of my academic transcript and also both work and academic references.
	IELTS 6	I have enclosed copies of my academic transcript as well as both academic and work-related references.
	IELTS 7+	Please find enclosed copies of my academic transcript as well as both academic and work-related references.
Sentence 6	IELTS 5	If you have any more questions about my study plans or background, you can contact me at the address or phone number at the top of the page.
	IELTS 6	Should you have any further questions about my study plans or background, please do not hesitate to contact me at the address or phone number provided above.
	IELTS 7+	Should you have any further queries regarding my study plans or background, please do not hesitate to contact me at the address or phone number provided above.

Academic Vocabulary 高分词汇

Basic 基础 informal	Intermediate 中级	Advanced 高级 formal
ask (v.)		enquire (v.)
have (v.) have got		hold (v.)
computer parts		computer components
but (adv./conj.)	however (adv./conj.)	
get (v.)		attain (v.)
enough (adj.)		sufficient (adj.)
about (prep.)		regarding (prep.) relating to
and (conj.)	along with/ as well as	
get in touch	contact (v.)	
at the top	above (prep.)	

Test Your Comprehension 综合练习

Answer these questions by circling A, B or C

1. Which is the best sentence to use in a formal letter (see both model answers)?
   A. I was wondering if this is likely to be sufficient?
   B. Is this good enough?
   C. I wonder if this is likely to be sufficient?

2. The word "***should***" (see Model Answer B) means:
   A. must
   B. a good idea
   C. if

3. Which of the following is only used in spoken English?
   A. have
   B. have got
   C. possess

4. What verb tense does the writer use to talk about his TOEFL score (see both model answers)?
   A. past simple tense
   B. present simple tense
   C. future simple tense

5. Which of the following sentences is grammatically wrong?
   A. I have not yet taken the IELTS test.
   B. I have not taken the IELTS test yet.
   C. I have yet not taken the IELTS test.

Answer these questions by writing YES or NO

6. The question asks you to write a formal letter.

7. "***To the Admissions Officer***" (see Model Answer A) is a good way to start a formal letter.

8. The phrase "***in order to***" (see Model Answer B) is used to explain why the writer is writing the letter.

9. The writer says he has put his contact details at the bottom of the page.

Check your answers

1. **A**
Past tense is more formal than present tense and direct questions are less formal.

2. **C**
"***Should***" has two meanings. It sometimes means that something is a good idea, and in formal writing sometimes means "***if***".

3. **B**
"***Have got***" is especially common in Australian and British English and is quite informal. Use it in speaking, but not in writing.

4. **A**
The writer took the TOEFL test in the past, so he uses past simple tense.

5. **C**
"***Yet***" can go at the end of the sentence or after "***not***".

6. **YES**

7. **NO**
You can write this on the outside of an envelope or package that you want to send, but not at the start of a letter.

8. **YES**
This is one of the most useful sentence structures in formal letter writing.

9. **NO**
The writer says he has put his contact details at the top of the page.

Question 27 Missed Immigration Interview
错过移民面谈

WRITING TASK 1

You should spend about 20 minutes on this task.

> ***You missed an appointment for an immigration interview recently because of circumstances out of your control.***
>
> ***Write to the immigration office. In your letter***
>
> - ***Introduce yourself***
> - ***Apologise for missing your appointment***
> - ***Explain what happened***
> - ***Request a new appointment***

Write at least 150 words.

You do **NOT** need to write any addresses.

Begin your letter as follows:

Dear ...,

Model Answer A: IELTS Band 5^+

Dear Keith,

I just want to explain why I couldn't make it to my immigration interview last Friday and arrange a new appointment. I was actually on my way to your office when I got a call from my daughter's school. Her teacher said she was having a bad asthma attack. Because my wife wasn't free at the time, I had to go to the hospital with my daughter. I tried to call your office to cancel the appointment, but then my mobile ran out of batteries. When I got to the hospital, I was busy taking care of my daughter and talking to the doctor so I just forgot. I'm really sorry for the trouble this probably caused the interviewer and your other staff. Could you please make a new appointment for me to have the interview within the next two weeks? I'm free before 12pm from Monday to Thursday and after 3pm on Friday. You can reach me at the address or phone number above. Thanks so much for your help.

Regards,
Vincent Lu

(176 words)

Model Answer B: IELTS Band 7^+

Dear Mr Wood,

I am writing in order to explain my absence from the immigration interview I was scheduled to attend last Friday and request a new appointment. I was, in fact, on my way to the interview when I received a call from my daughter's school saying that she was suffering a severe asthma attack. As my wife was not available, it was necessary for me to accompany my daughter to the hospital. I then attempted to contact your office to cancel my appointment; however, my mobile phone ran out of batteries. Once at the hospital, I was busy comforting my daughter and talking to the doctor so I simply forgot. I sincerely apologise for the inconvenience I am sure I caused the interviewer and others at your office. I was wondering if it would be possible to arrange a new appointment for sometime during the next two weeks? I am available until 12pm from Monday to Thursday and after 3pm on Friday and can be contacted at the e-mail address or phone number provided. I appreciate your assistance in this matter.

Yours sincerely,
Vincent Lu

(187 words)

Model Sentence Structures 句型示范

Sentence 1	IELTS 5	I just wanted to explain why I couldn't make it to my immigration interview last Friday and ask for a new appointment.
	IELTS 6	I am writing to explain why I was absent from the immigration interview I was scheduled to attend last Friday and ask for a new appointment.
	IELTS 7+	I am writing in order to explain my absence from the immigration interview I was scheduled to attend last Friday and request a new appointment.
Sentence 2	IELTS 5	Because my wife wasn't free at the time, I had to go to the hospital with my daughter.
	IELTS 6	As my wife was not free at the time, I needed to accompany my daughter to the hospital.
	IELTS 7+	As my wife was not available, it was necessary for me to accompany my daughter to the hospital.
Sentence 3	IELTS 6	When I got to the hospital, I was busy taking care of my daughter and talking to the doctor so I just forgot.
	IELTS 7+	Once at the hospital, I was busy comforting my daughter and talking to the doctor so I simply forgot.
Sentence 4	IELTS 5	I'm really sorry for the trouble this probably caused the interviewer and your other staff.
	IELTS 6	I sincerely apologise for the trouble I am sure I caused the interviewer and others at your office.
	IELTS 7+	I sincerely apologise for the inconvenience I am sure I caused the interviewer and others at your office.

Sentence 5	**IELTS 5**	Could you please make a new appointment for me to have the interview within the next two weeks?
	IELTS 6	I was wondering if you could arrange a new appointment for sometime within the next two weeks?
	IELTS 7+	I was wondering if it would be possible to arrange a new appointment for sometime during the next two weeks?
Sentence 6	**IELTS 5**	I'm free before 12pm from Monday to Thursday and after 3pm on Friday. You can reach me at the address or phone number above.
	IELTS 6	I am free before 12pm from Monday to Thursday and after 3pm on Friday. You can contact me at the e-mail address or phone number provided.
	IELTS 7+	I am available until 12pm from Monday to Thursday and after 3pm on Friday and can be contacted at the e-mail address or phone number provided.

Academic Vocabulary 高分词汇

Basic 基础 informal	Intermediate 中级	Advanced 高级 formal
make it		attend (v.)
actually (adv.)	in fact	
get (v.)	receive (v.)	
have (an illness)		suffer (an illness)
because (conj.)		as (conj.)
	free (adj.)	available (adj.)
go with	accompany (v.)	
try (v.)		attempt (n./v.)
call (n./v.)	contact (n./v.) reach (v.)	
but (adv./conj.)	however (adv./conj.)	
just (adv.)		simply (adv.)
trouble (n./v.)	inconvenience (n./v.)	
before (prep.)	until (prep.)	
help (n./v.)		assistance (n.)

Test Your Comprehension 综合练习

Answer these questions by circling A, B or C

Question 1 refers to the following four simplified sentences taken from the model answers.

> **i. My daughter had a serious asthma attack and my wife was not available at the time.**
> **ii. Could you arrange a new appointment for me sometime during the next two weeks?**
> **iii. I am writing in order to explain why I missed my immigration interview last Friday.**
> **iv. Hence, I had to go to the hospital with my daughter.**

1. Put the above sentences in the correct order.
   A. iii. / i. / iv. / ii.
   B. iv. / ii. / iii. / i.
   C. iii. / i. / ii. / iv.

2. Question 27 asks you to:
   A. apologise for being late to an interview, explain what happened and request a new appointment
   B. say sorry for missing an interview, explain what happened and ask for a new appointment
   C. explain why you missed your appointment

3. The writer says he missed his immigration interview because:
   A. his daughter was sick
   B. his wife was busy
   C. both of the above

Answer these questions by writing YES or NO

4. Question 27 asks you to write to a person called Keith Wood.

5. The writer uses present tense to talk about his daughter's asthma attack (see both model answers).

6. This is an informal letter.

7. It is better to use a person's surname (family name) when you start a formal letter.

8. You can use the word "***suffer***" (see Model Answer B) to talk about any illness or injury.

9. "***I'm sorry***" (see Model Answer A) is less formal than "***I sincerely apologise***" (see Model Answer B).

10. The word "***once***" (see Model Answer B) has two meanings: it sometimes means "***one time***" and sometimes means "***after***".

Check your answers

1. **A**
   Sentences have a logical order. Your writing must be logical if you want the reader to understand you.

2. **B**

3. **C**
   The writer's daughter had an asthma attack and his wife was not available.

4. **NO**
   But you can invent names.

5. **NO**
   The writer uses past tense.

6. **NO**
   This is a formal letter.

7. **YES**
   If you know a person's surname, use it.

8. **YES**
   We often use the word "***suffer***" when we want to talk about a negative experience.

9. **YES**
   "***I sincerely apologise***" is better in a formal letter.

10. **YES**
    "***Once***" can mean "***one time***" or "***after***".

Informal Letter
非正式信件

Question 28 Saying Goodbye
道别

WRITING TASK 1

You should spend about 20 minutes on this task.

You recently finished studying at a university in another country where you shared a house with a fellow student. Something urgent came up while your housemate was away on a short trip and you had to leave without saying goodbye.

Write to your housemate. In your letter

- ***Apologise for leaving without saying goodbye***
- ***Explain why you had to leave***

Write at least 150 words.

You do **NOT** need to write any addresses.

Begin your letter as follows:

Dear ...,

Model Answer A: IELTS Band 5^+ (too formal)

Dear Ms Carruthers,

I am writing with regard to my unexplained early departure, for which I must apologise. Unforeseen and pressing matters arose at home—my grandmother fell ill and was hospitalised. She has since fully recovered though. I trust you had a pleasant holiday and would like to hear more about it if you have time to write. I believe you have my e-mail address, so perhaps in addition you could forward some photographs. I placed some money on the refrigerator as a contribution towards last month's telephone and electricity bills. Please do not hesitate to contact me should this prove insufficient. If you are not otherwise occupied perhaps you could visit me during the winter break. You could make use of our vacant guest room. I would most enjoy showing you the sights of Beijing. Lastly, please allow me to express my gratitude to you for being such a wonderful housemate—your tolerance of my untidiness and frequent bad moods was greatly appreciated. It is my sincere hope that we can maintain contact in the future. Please keep my invitation for the winter holidays in mind.

Yours sincerely,
Rachel Liang

(192 words)

Model Answer B: IELTS Band 7^+

Dear Joanne,

Sorry I had to leave in such a hurry without saying goodbye. Something urgent came up at home—my grandmother got sick and had to be taken to hospital. Everything's fine now though. Anyway, I hope you had a nice holiday. Please write and tell me about it if you've got the time. You have my e-mail address, so maybe you could send some photos too. I also hope you found the money for the phone and electricity bills that I left on the fridge—let me know if it's not enough. Actually, I was thinking that if you're not doing anything else, maybe you could come and visit me during the winter break. You could stay in the guest room here—I'd really love to show you the sights of Beijing. Anyway, I just wanted to say how much I've enjoyed being your housemate. I know I can be a bit messy at times, not to mention cranky, so thanks for putting up with me. Well, I'd better be going now. Keep in touch and don't forget my invitation for the winter holidays.

Regards,
Rachel

(191 words)

Model Sentence Structures 句型示范

Sentence 1	**IELTS 5**	I am writing with regard to my unexplained early departure, for which I must apologise.
	IELTS 6	I am writing to apologise for my unexplained early departure.
	IELTS 7+	Sorry I had to leave in such a hurry without saying goodbye.
Sentence 2	**IELTS 5**	Unforeseen and pressing matters arose at home—my grandmother fell ill and was hospitalised.
	IELTS 6	Something unforeseen and pressing came up at home—my grandmother fell ill and was taken to hospital.
	IELTS 7+	Something urgent came up at home—my grandmother got sick and had to be taken to hospital.
Sentence 3	**IELTS 5**	I trust you had a pleasant holiday and would like to hear more about it if you have time to write.
	IELTS 6	I trust you had a nice holiday and would like to hear about it if you have time to write.
	IELTS 7+	I hope you had a nice holiday. Please write and tell me about it if you've got the time.

Sentence 4	**IELTS 5**	I placed some money on the refrigerator as a contribution towards last month's telephone and electricity bills. Please do not hesitate to contact me should this prove insufficient.
	IELTS 6	I also hope you found the money I placed on the refrigerator as a contribution towards last month's telephone and electricity bills—please do not hesitate to contact me if this is insufficient.
	IELTS 7^+	I also hope you found the money for the phone and electricity bills that I left on the fridge—let me know if it's not enough.
Sentence 5	**IELTS 6**	If you are not otherwise occupied perhaps you could visit me during the winter break.
	IELTS 7^+	If you're not doing anything else, maybe you could come and visit me during the winter break.
Sentence 6	**IELTS 5**	Lastly, please allow me to express my gratitude to you for being such a wonderful housemate—your tolerance of my untidiness and frequent bad moods was greatly appreciated.
	IELTS 6	Lastly, I just wanted to express my thanks to you for being such a wonderful housemate. I really appreciated the fact that you were so tolerant, because I know I can be quite untidy at times, not to mention bad-tempered.
	IELTS 7^+	Anyway, I just wanted to say how much I've enjoyed being your housemate. I know I can be a bit messy at times, not to mention cranky, so thanks for putting up with me.

Academic Vocabulary 高分词汇

Basic 基础 informal	Intermediate 中级	Advanced 高级 formal
leave (v.)		depart (v.)
		urgent (adj.) pressing (adj.)
come up		arise (v.)
get sick		fall ill
nice (adj.)		pleasant (adj.)
maybe (adv.)		perhaps (adv.)
send (v.)		forward (v.)
too (adv.)	in addition	
photo (n.)	photograph (n./v.)	
fridge (n.)	refrigerator (n.)	
not enough		insufficient (adj.)
break (n.)	holiday (n.)	
love (v.)	enjoy (v.)	
messy (adj.)	untidy (adj.)	
	put up with	tolerate (v.)
	keep in touch	maintain contact

Test Your Comprehension 综合练习

Answer these questions by circling A, B or C

1. Question 28 asks you to write a letter to:
   A. someone you know well
   B. someone you have met but do not know well
   C. a total stranger

2. So this letter should be written in:
   A. formal English
   B. informal English
   C. British English

3. Which of the following sentences is too formal for this letter?
   A. It is my sincere hope that we can maintain contact in the future.
   B. Keep in touch.
   C. Don't be a stranger.

4. The word "***anyway***" (see Model Answer B) is usually used in:
   A. formal English
   B. informal English
   C. both

Answer these questions by writing YES or NO

5. You can use a person's first name in informal letters (see Model Answer B).

6. "***Actually***" (see Model Answer B) is a good word to use in this letter because it is informal.

7. You can use contractions like "***you've***" and "***it's***" (see Model Answer B) in this kind of informal letter.

8. "***Keep my invitation ... in mind***" (see Model Answer A) means "***don't forget my invitation***" (see Model Answer B).

9. The word "***untidiness***" (see Model Answer A) is the adjective for "***untidy***".

10. In this letter, it is best to sign off with "***Yours sincerely***" because you know the other person's name.

Check your answers

1. **A**
   You probably know your housemate quite well.

2. **B**
   This is a personal letter to someone you know well, so it is informal.

3. **A**
   This is a very long and complicated way to say something simple. You only need to use this kind of English in formal letter writing.

4. **B**
   "***Anyway***" is commonly used in speaking.

5. **YES**
   "***Dear Joanne***" is the best way to start because this is a personal letter. Make up names if you need to.

6. **YES**
   "***Actually***" is a great word to use in speaking and informal writing.

7. **YES**
   You can use contractions in speaking or informal writing.

8. **YES**
   "***Keep in mind***" means "***don't forget***".

9. **NO**
   "***Untidiness***" is a noun; "***untidy***" is an adjective.

10. **NO**
    "***Yours sincerely***" is too formal here. "***Regards***" is better.

Question 29 In Hospital 住院

WRITING TASK 1

You should spend about 20 minutes on this task.

You are in hospital as a result of a recent accident. Your co-workers have visited you several times and have given you cards and flowers.

Write to your workmates. In your letter

- ***Tell them about your current condition***
- ***Thank them for their thoughts and support***

Write at least 150 words.

You do **NOT** need to write any addresses.

Begin your letter as follows:

Dear ...,

Model Answer A: IELTS Band 5⁺ (too formal)

To Whom It May Concern,

I am writing in order to express my heartfelt appreciation for all the cards, flowers, phone calls and visits I have received since my accident. The concern you have all shown has been moving. I also wish to inform you that my condition has vastly improved, despite the agony that my daily physiotherapy exercises still cause me. The doctor seems confident that I will be able to return home in the very near future. Were I able to do so, I would check out immediately as I am finding the monotony of daytime television unbearable. Hospitals can be incredibly boring places, particularly when one is confined to bed with one's leg suspended in a sling. Although I frequently express my displeasure at how busy we constantly are with overtime and meetings, I now have a far greater appreciation for my job and am eagerly anticipating my return to work. I trust you are all in good health. Thank you once again for your care and consideration. I look forward to seeing you all soon.

Yours faithfully,
Ivan Tang

(183 words)

Model Answer B: IELTS Band 7⁺

Dear Friends,

Thank you all so much for your cards, flowers, phone calls and visits since my accident. Your care and concern mean a lot to me. I'm feeling much better today, although the exercises I have to do are really painful. The doctor says I can probably go home in a few days' time. To tell the truth, I'd check out today if I could—I'm already sick to death of daytime TV. Hospitals can be such boring places, especially when your leg is hanging in a sling and you can't leave your bed. I know I always complain about how busy we are with overtime and meetings and everything, but now I realise how much I actually enjoy my job. I just want to get back on my feet and back to work as soon as I can. Anyway, I hope you are all well. Thanks again and I hope to see you all very soon.

Regards,
Ivan

(160 words)

Model Sentence Structures 句型示范

Sentence 1	**IELTS 5**	I am writing in order to express my heartfelt appreciation for all the cards, flowers, phone calls and visits I have received since my accident.
	IELTS 6	I am writing to say thank-you for all the cards, flowers, phone calls and visits I have gotten since my accident.
	IELTS 7⁺	Thank you all so much for your cards, flowers, phone calls and visits since my accident.
Sentence 2	**IELTS 5**	I also wish to inform you that my condition has vastly improved, despite the agony that my daily physiotherapy exercises still cause me.
	IELTS 6	I also wanted to tell you that my condition has greatly improved, although my daily physiotherapy exercises still cause me a lot of pain.
	IELTS 7⁺	I'm feeling much better today, although the exercises I have to do are really painful.
Sentence 3	**IELTS 5**	The doctor seems confident that I will be able to return home in the very near future.
	IELTS 6	The doctor says he is confident that I will be able to go home soon.
	IELTS 7⁺	The doctor says I can probably go home in a few days' time.

Sentence 4	**IELTS 5**	Were I able to do so, I would check out immediately as I am finding the monotony of daytime television unbearable.
	IELTS 6	If I could, I would check out immediately as I'm finding daytime television incredibly boring.
	IELTS 7+	I'd check out today if I could—I'm already sick to death of daytime TV.
Sentence 5	**IELTS 6**	Hospitals can be incredibly boring places, particularly when one is confined to bed with one's leg suspended in a sling.
	IELTS 7+	Hospitals can be such boring places, especially when your leg is hanging in a sling and you can't leave your bed.
Sentence 6	**IELTS 5**	Although I frequently express my displeasure at how busy we constantly are with overtime and meetings, I now have a far greater appreciation for my job.
	IELTS 6	Although I often complain about how busy we always are with overtime and meetings, I now have a much greater appreciation for my job.
	IELTS 7+	I know I always complain about how busy we are with overtime and meetings and everything, but now I realise how much I actually enjoy my job.

Academic Vocabulary 高分词汇

Basic 基础 informal	**Intermediate** 中级	**Advanced** 高级 formal
	although (conj.)	despite (prep.)
	pain (n.)	agony (n.)
	painful (adj.)	agonising (adj.)
can (aux. v.)		(be) able to
go home	return home	
actually (adv.) to tell the truth		
TV (n.)	television (n.)	
boring (adj.)		monotonous (adj.)
boredom (n.)		monotony (n.)
		especially (adv.) particularly (adv.)
hanging (adj.)		suspended (adj.)
*always (adv.)		constantly (adv.) frequently (adv.)
complain (v.)		express displeasure
enjoy (v.)		appreciate (v.)
enjoyment (n.)		appreciation (n.)
look forward to		eagerly anticipate
hope (n./v.)		trust (n./v.)
soon (adv.)		in the very near future

Note: Sometimes the word "always" is used to mean "frequently" or "often". This is called exaggeration or hyperbole. For example: "My football team always wins!"

Test Your Comprehension 综合练习

Answer these questions by circling A, B or C

1. Question 29 asks you to write:
   A. a formal letter of thanks
   B. an informal letter of thanks
   C. an informal letter of apology

2. In Question 29 the recipients of the letter are your:
   A. colleagues
   B. classmates
   C. friends

3. The word "***such***" (see Model Answer B) is followed by:
   A. a noun
   B. an adjective
   C. an adjective and then a noun

4. The writer starts and finishes this letter by saying:
   A. why he is writing
   B. his name
   C. thank you

Answer these questions by writing YES or NO

5. "***Dear Friends***" (see Model Answer B) is a good way to start a letter to a group of people you know quite well.

6. "***I trust***" (see Model Answer A) is a more formal way to write "***I hope***" (see Model Answer B).

7. The writer uses "***would***" and "***could***" in the phrase "***I'd check out today if I could***" (see Model Answer B) because it is impossible.

8. The writer mainly uses past tense in these letters (see both model answers).

9. "***Get back on my feet***" (see Model Answer B) means "***walk again***".

10. "***Yours faithfully***" is too formal for this letter.

Check your answers

1. **B**

2. **A**

   "***Colleague***" is the same as "***workmate***" or "***co-worker***". Your colleagues may be your friends, but not necessarily.

3. **C**

   You should know how to change the sentence, "***Hospitals are such boring places***" into "***Hospitals are so boring***".

4. **C**

   It is sometimes good to start and finish a letter by saying thank you.

5. **YES**

6. **YES**

   "***Trust***" has two meanings. It sometimes means "***believe***" and sometimes means "***hope***".

7. **YES**

   "***Would***" and "***could***" are often used to talk about impossible or imaginary actions.

8. **NO**

   The writer uses present tense.

9. **NO**

   "***Get back on my feet***" means "***get well***" or "***recover***".

10. **YES**

    "***Yours faithfully***" is for formal letter writing.

Question 30 Change of Plans 计划变更

WRITING TASK 1

You should spend about 20 minutes on this task.

An old friend of yours is coming to visit your city. You had planned to meet him at the airport, but something has come up and you will not be able to make it there on time.

Write to your friend. In your letter

- ***Explain the situation***
- ***Offer to make alternate arrangements***

Write at least 150 words.

You do **NOT** need to write any addresses.

Begin your letter as follows:

Dear ...,

Model Answer A: IELTS Band 5$^+$ (too formal)

Dear Mr. Mason,

This letter concerns your upcoming visit to Beijing. I trust that preparations are progressing without hindrance. Based on past experience, I presume that you have yet to begin packing. I am eagerly anticipating your visit and have already conducted all the preparations necessary for you to make use of my guest room. Unfortunately, though, it will no longer be possible for me to be present for your arrival at 11:45 as I had initially planned since I will be required to attend a meeting that morning. If you have no objection to waiting it may be possible for me to reach the airport by approximately 13:30. If such a delay would be unacceptable to you, however, I will make arrangements for my secretary to meet you at the airport and accompany you to my residence. Kindly provide instructions in this regard prior to your departure and, as always, do not hesitate to contact me at the address and phone number provided should you require any further assistance.

Yours faithfully,
Zhu, Chen Yi
(175 words)

Model Answer B: IELTS Band 7+

Dear Jason,

I hope you're well and preparations for your visit to Beijing are going smoothly. If I know you, you probably haven't even started packing yet. I'm really looking forward to seeing you again and have already prepared the guest room for you. I have some bad news though—I will not be able to meet you at the airport when you arrive at 11:45 as I had originally planned. Unfortunately, I have to go to a meeting on the morning you get here, but if you don't mind waiting I could probably make it by about 13:30. If that doesn't suit you, I could send my secretary to meet you instead. Anyway, please let me know which you prefer sometime before you leave. Well, I guess that's about all I needed to say. You've got my number, so give me a call if there's anything else you need to know. Take care of yourself, and I'll see you when you get here.

Kind regards,
Chen Yi
(168 words)

Model Sentence Structures 句型示范

Sentence 1	IELTS 5	This letter concerns your upcoming visit to Beijing.
	IELTS 6	This letter is about your approaching visit to Beijing.
	IELTS 7+	I'm writing about your visit to Beijing.
Sentence 2	IELTS 6	I trust that you are well and that preparations are progressing without hindrance.
	IELTS 7+	I hope you're well and preparations for your visit to Beijing are going smoothly.
Sentence 3	IELTS 5	Based on past experience, I presume you have yet to begin packing.
	IELTS 6	Based on past experience, I presume you have not begun packing yet.
	IELTS 7+	If I know you, you probably haven't even started packing yet.
Sentence 4	IELTS 5	I am eagerly anticipating your visit and have already conducted all the preparations necessary for you to make use of my guest room.
	IELTS 6	I am really looking forward to your visit and have already made all the preparations necessary for you to use the guest room.
	IELTS 7+	I'm really looking forward to seeing you again and have already prepared the guest room for you.

Sentence 5	**IELTS 5**	Unfortunately, though, it will no longer be possible for me to be present for your arrival at 11:45 as I had initially planned since I will be required to attend a meeting that morning.
	IELTS 6	Unfortunately, though, I will not be able to be there at the airport for your arrival at 11:45 as I had originally planned because I have to attend a meeting that morning.
	IELTS 7+	I have some bad news though—I will not be able to meet you at the airport when you arrive at 11:45 as I had originally planned. Unfortunately, I have to go to a meeting on the morning you get here.
Sentence 6	**IELTS 5**	Kindly provide instructions in this regard prior to your departure.
	IELTS 6	Kindly give me instructions in this regard before your departure.
	IELTS 7+	Anyway, please let me know which you prefer sometime before you leave.

Academic Vocabulary 高分词汇

Basic 基础 informal	Intermediate 中级	Advanced 高级 formal
hope (n./v.)		trust (n./v.)
	smoothly (adv.)	without hindrance
look forward to		eagerly anticipate
	prepare (v.)	conduct preparations
	originally (adv.)	initially (adv.)
have to		(be) required to
go to		attend (v.)
don't mind		have no objection
make it		reach (v.)
about (adv.)		approximately (adv.)
please (adv.)		kindly (adv.)
let me know		provide instructions
before (prep.)		prior to
leave (v.)		depart (v.)
need (n./v.)		require (v.)

Test Your Comprehension 综合练习

Answer these questions by circling A, B or C

1. Question 30 asks you to write:
   A. a formal letter explaining a change of plans
   B. an informal letter of apology
   C. an informal letter explaining a change of plans

2. In this letter, you should greet the recipient using his/her:
   A. nickname
   B. surname
   C. first name

3. A "***hindrance***" (see Model Answer A) is something that:
   A. helps you
   B. stops you or slows you down
   C. makes you sick

4. "***Will not be able to***" (see Model Answer B) is the future tense of:
   A. would not
   B. must not
   C. can not

Answer these questions by writing YES or NO

5. Model Answer A is better than Model Answer B because it is longer.

6. You can use a dash (—) to join two sentences if the second sentence explains something about the first one (see Model Answer B).

7. "***Such a delay***" (see Model Answer A) means "***this kind of delay***".

8. "***Though***" (see Model Answer A) can mean "***however***".

9. "***Kind regards***" is a good way to sign off on an informal letter.

Check your answers

1. **C**

2. **C**

3. **B**
A "***hindrance***" is a "***barrier***" or "***obstacle***".

4. **C**
The past tense is "***could not***"; the present tense is "***cannot***"; and the future tense is "***will not be able to***".

5. **NO**
Model Answer B is better even though it is shorter, because it uses the right level of English (the correct register).

6. **YES**
Punctuation is an important part of good writing. You should try not to always use the same punctuation—learn some different ways to punctuate a sentence.

7. **YES**

8. **YES**
"***Though***" can replace "***however***" in the middle of a sentence or at the end, but not at the beginning.

9. **YES**
You can use "***Kind regards***" if you know the other person quite well, but you are not very close. You would probably not write it to your best friend.

A Few Final Tips

How to Approach IELTS IELTS 高分小秘诀

In order to succeed in IELTS writing, it is vital that you think about your own attitude very carefully, because attitude is something that prevents many candidates from getting the score that they need. However, if you think about IELTS the right way, you will be one of the candidates who learns quickly and gets a higher score. Remember…

1. Be realistic! 实际一点！

Learning a language is hard work. Anyone who thinks they can improve their English from "***Hello, my name is Jack!***" to postgraduate university level in one or two months is dreaming. There is no magic formula that can give you really good English overnight. Give yourself enough time to prepare.

学习语言是相当艰辛的，没有人可以一步登天或才学一两个月英文就能书写流利、出口成章。准备IELTS没有捷径，要给自己留出充分的时间。

2. Do not give up too easily! 别轻言放弃！

You may be quite optimistic when you start preparing for IELTS, then feel disappointed and let down when you find out how difficult it really is. Do not quit! It is just a matter of time and effort. You can do it if you set your mind to it.

在准备IELTS的过程中，你可能会发现IELTS很难而想中途放弃，千万别这么做，只要持续练习，你就会有所收获。

3. Do not be scared to make mistakes. 别怕犯错。

You may be scared to speak or write because you do not want people to laugh at you when you make mistakes. But in language learning mistakes are actually good because they are opportunities to improve. If you want to learn, you need to be brave and take risks. Speak up in class and do not be scared to start a conversation with an English speaker.

学英文时你可能常害怕犯错会招来别人的嘲笑，而不敢开口讲英文或动笔写英文；然而，犯错其实是在积累经验，会促进英文进步。不要害怕会犯错，勇于开口说英文才会进步。

4. Ask the right questions. 问对问题。

There is an old saying in English: If you ask a silly question, you get a silly answer. Many candidates ask their teachers silly questions that have no answer. If you ask "***How can I get a better score in IELTS?***" you will get a very vague answer that will not help you at all. But if you ask "***How can I write an introduction to an essay about a pie chart?***" the answer you get may be very useful indeed.

学英文要问对问题，英文才会进步。例如"怎样才能在IELTS测试中取得高分?"这样的问题太笼统，你可能也不会得到什么好答案。而"图表题的开头要怎么写?"这样的问题，就可能帮你提高英文成绩。

5. Use the same material several times. 重复利用参考资料。

It is good to review the same IELTS material more than once to make sure that you have really learnt it. Do not always look for new material when you have not learnt everything you can from the old material yet. Your score does not depend on how many IELTS books you read (or how many classes you go to). Quality is more important than quantity.

不需要一直更换新的IELTS考试用书，学透已有的材料更重要，质量重于数量。

6. Do not just memorise lots of vocabulary. 不要只背单词。

Yes, vocabulary is important, but when you learn a word you should make sure you know it well. You must know how to spell it; you must know other forms of the word (E.g. "***high***" and "***height***"); and you must know whether the word is used in spoken English or in writing (E.g. "***get***" and "***gain***"). It will help you more if you learn a few words really well and then learn different sentences and language patterns that you can use them in. Look at this example:

Regular exercise offers tremendous health benefits.

Many candidates would look at this sentence and decide to learn the word "***tremendous***". However, I think it is much more important for you to learn that "***offer benefits***" is a common phrase in English and that we often use "***tremendous***" together with "***benefits***".

没错，单词很重要，但你必须真正地学会如何使用它，学会它的各种词性变化，还要能在英文口语或写作中运用。从句子中学单词和句型，比猛背一个一个的单词有用多了。

Improve Your Spelling 拼写正误表

The list below contains words that Chinese IELTS candidates often spell wrongly. Make sure you can spell these words correctly first, then keep a record of any other spelling mistakes you make as you prepare for the exam and review it regularly so that you do not repeat the same ones again. The secret to improving your spelling is to make sure that every mistake you make is a new mistake. Obviously, you will need a teacher to help check your writing for spelling errors. DO NOT write practice essays on a computer using a spell checker! Use a pen and paper.

Wrong!	Right!
affection	affect (v.) / effect (n.)
althought	although
arguement	argument
Chiness	Chinese
convinence	convenience
convient	convenient
crimer	criminal
destory	destroy
droped	dropped (past tense of "***drop***")
goverment	government
endangerous species	endangered species
eniverment	environment
flucturate	fluctuate
forign	foreign
graphy	graph
materil	material
morden	modern
nagative	negative
unclear energy	nuclear energy
opion	opinion

precentage	percentage
perhapes	perhaps
propotion	proportion
sitution	situation
slove	solve
tranditional	traditional
undergroung	underground
unempolyed	unemployed
varity	variety
vertial axis	vertical axis
worldwild	worldwide

读者反馈表

尊敬的读者：

您好！非常感谢您对**新东方大愚图书**的信赖与支持，希望您抽出宝贵的时间填写这份反馈表，以便帮助我们改进工作，今后能为您提供更优秀的图书。谢谢！

为了答谢您对我们的支持，我们将对反馈的信息进行随机抽奖活动，当月将有20位幸运读者可获赠**《新东方英语》**期刊一份。我们将定期在新东方大愚图书网站 www.dogwood.com.cn 公布获奖者名单并及时寄出奖品，敬请关注。

来信请寄： 北京市海淀区海淀中街6号新东方大厦750室　北京新东方大愚文化传播有限公司

图书部收

邮编：100080　　E-mail：club@dogwood.com.cn

姓名：________　年龄：________　职业：________　教育背景：________　邮编：________

通讯地址：________________________　联系电话：________

E-mail：____________　您所购买的书籍的名称是：____________

1. 您是通过何种渠道得知本书的（可多选）：
   □书店　□新东方网站　□大愚网站　□朋友推荐　□老师推荐　□其他________
2. 您是从何处购买到此书的？　□书店　□邮购　□图书销售网站　□其他________
3. 影响您购买此书的原因（可多选）：
   □封面设计　□书评广告　□正文内容　□图书价格　□新东方品牌　□新东方名师　□其他________
4. 您对本书的封面设计满意程度：　□很满意　□比较满意　□一般　□不满意　□改进建议________
5. 本书配哪种音像资料更适合您？　□磁带　□光盘　□MP3　□其他________
6. 您认为本书的内文在哪些方面还需改进？　□结构编排　□难易程度　□内容丰富性　□内文版式
7. 本书最令您满意的地方：□内文　□封面　□价格　□纸张
8. 您对本书的推荐率：□没有　□1人　□1－3人　□3－5人　□5人以上
9. 您更希望我们为您提供哪些方面的英语类图书？
   □四六级类　□考研类　□雅思考试类　□GRE、GMAT类　□NEW SAT类　□实用商务类
   □休闲欣赏类　□初高中英语类　□其他________
   您目前最希望我们为您出版的图书名称是：________
10. 您在学习英语过程中最需要哪些方面的帮助？（可多选）
    □词汇　□听力　□口语　□阅读　□写作　□翻译　□其他
11. 您最喜欢的英语图书品牌：________
    理由如下（可多选）：□版式漂亮　□内容实用　□难度适宜　□价格适中　□对考试有帮助　□其他________
12. 看到"新东方"三个字，您首先想到什么？________
13. 您的其他意见和建议（可附在本页背面）：________
14. 填表时间：______ 年 ____ 月 ___ 日